SACRED COWS DANCING
Volume 1, Financial Enlightenment For Today

SACRED COWS DANCING
Volume 1, Financial Enlightenment For Today

Dr. Houston Vetter

with
Dr. Joe Vitale & Pat O'Bryan

also with
Jerry Stocking, Morty Lefkoe, Dr. Joe Rubino,
John La Valle, Connie Ragen Green,
Wendy Down, & Geoff Hoff

Portable Empire Publishing, 2011

Copyright © 2011 Houston Vetter. All rights reserved.
Author photo: Lee Rodriguez Photographers 713-861-7844
Cover illustration: ICLIPART

ISBN 978-0-9836900-3-0

Published by Portable Empire Publishing, Wimberley, Texas For more information, or to learn how you can publish *your* book, visit www.PortableEmpirePublishing.com.

No part of this publication may be reproduced, stored in a retrieval system, or transmitted in any form or by any means, electronic, mechanical, photocopying, recording, scanning, or otherwise, except as permitted under Section 107 or 108 of the 1976 United States Copyright Act, without the prior written permission of the publisher or copyright holder. Requests to the publisher should be addressed to Portable Empire Publishing, PO Box 2272, Wimberley, Texas 78676. Requests to the copyright holder at Houston Vetter, 12046 N. Fairhollow Lane, Houston, Texas 77043.

Limit of Liability/Disclaimer of Warranty: The publisher, designers, contributors, editors, and author have used their best efforts in preparing this book, they make no warranties or representations with respect to the accuracy or completeness of the contents of this book and specifically disclaim any implied warranties of merchantability or finances for a particular purpose. It is further acknowledged that no warranty, of any kind, may be created or extended by any written sales materials or sales representatives. The advice and strategies contained herein may not be suitable for your situation and do contain risk including the risk of financial loss. You should always consult with a financial or legal professional where appropriate before undertaking any action and users of this material assume all risk. Neither the publisher, designers, editors, contributors nor the author shall be liable for any loss of profit or any other commercial damages, including but not limited to financial, special, incidental, consequential, or other damages.

CONTENTS

1	Author's Foreword
5	How to Use This Book
9	Presuppositions
15	The BS Factor About Money
21	The Money Rant And More BS Factor
29	Choosing Your Own Target
39	Eye of the Needle, or, The Shocking Spiritual Truth About Money
47	The Inside Scoop! Subjectivity Inside Objectivity for Business
53	How You Can Eliminate Beliefs For Good
61	How Much is that Doggie in the Window? The Myth of Money
69	Are You Acting from Gratitude, Love, and Trust or Doubt and Fear?
75	The Myth of Inspiration, the Non-Metaphysical Side of Law of Attraction and Getting Things Done

83	Blame, Shame, Guilt and Responsibility; It Is Really A Math Problem
87	Success and Your Life
91	Want to Make More Money Last Year?
101	The Root of All Evil
109	The Easiest Way To Have Money Flow To You
115	Conclusion
117	Testimonials
123	Resources
125	About the Author

Author's Foreword

When this all started out and I got the inspiration to write a book called *Sacred Cows Dancing* I thought originally it would be about combining Spirituality, Religion, Business and Family along with health, fitness and finances in a way where people would see the connection between everything and how they are different aspects of the same coin called Life. And also, open the door to the understanding that all of Life is Spiritual even when we call it something else like worldly or earthly or flesh or bad or physical or material. It is all the extension of Spirit.

That word (Spirit) may not sit right with you or it may and just in case it doesn't let's use the word energy as it may not have as much of an emotional charge to it. For the purposes of this book we are going to use the idea that everything is made up of energy. For this model there is nothing outside of energy and all there is, is energy. Everything is made up of energy and energy holds, interpenetrates and surrounds everything.

(To some people this might sound like a description of

God, Source, Unconditional Love, Universe, The Void, Spirit, Nothingness, Tao, etc, so please bear with me in this as using the word energy has less emotional charge to it than using the term God or universe, etc. as people often have an emotional charge around terms that hold religious connotations.) As my Grampa Vetter would say, "In the beginning God created man in his own image and ever since man's been returning the favor." So by using, a more neutral term "energy" it gives us the chance to see things in a more useful light.

As I spent the time to find out what and where inspiration was carrying me with *Sacred Cows Dancing* I simply made sure I was open to the leading of where the energy was going. If I tried to write in one direction and it felt like a chore I'd stop because the resistance let me know I was working from motivation instead of inspiration. Motivation isn't bad, it's just that it takes a lot more work to use motivation than inspiration and now-a-days I am paying more and more attention to the path of least resistance because things really are meant to work out easily, quickly and smoothly for each and every one of us.

As inspiration lead me to understand, by dealing mainly with the subject of money, it is a metaphor for all the other areas I had hoped to address in this book. Inspiration lead me to asked some of my friends to contribute chapters to this work and since I've gotten the different chapters from the different authors now I understand (a little better) what's going on.

This book is written in a way that no matter where you are on the continuum of Spiritual to Physical there is something in this book that can encourage you to your own inspiration. The thing I like about this book is, because of the way it is put together it is a flexible book. Most of us have heard the old saying that when the student is ready the teacher will appear. Well the truth of the matter is we are always being taught and we may not be aware of who the teacher is. And something that at one time did not make sense when read later, makes perfect sense now.

I remember the day, back when I was a pastor for a non-denominational church, that I realized I had learned all I could learn from a particular teacher. It wasn't that he was good, bad, right or wrong. I just knew in my knower that I had absorbed all the wisdom I was going to receive from this particular teacher. I was not anger, upset, sad or hurt. It was as if I was saying goodbye to a favorite teacher. He had pointed me in the direction to go and he was no longer needed.

Others came along who refined what I had learned from this teacher which led me further and deeper into wisdom and how things worked. Now some of these later teachers if I had attempted to learn from them first I would have been sorely disappointed. Because I did not have a solid enough foundation to be able to incorporate and use the new knowledge I was getting from these later teachers.

Well this book is sorta that way. The only difference

is all the levels of teaching from foundation to mansion building are in these pages. Some of the ways are harder and some are easier. And when you read it, some parts of it you will resonate with and other parts you may not. But that is something to get excited about because the next time you read this book you will be delighted to find that what you used to resonate with may still have some energy and yet now you find you resonate a lot more with other sections that before you did not resonate with and you will find money and other things that you want showing up in your life more often with less effort.

This is something to celebrate because it simply indicates that your quote "energy vibration" is rising. Or your frequencies are moving to the place where you do less and get more of everything, including money.

I want you to understand that wherever you are and whatever you resonate with in this book and what you don't resonate with is perfectly OK. You are not wrong and you don't have to work really hard to change it. Simply noticing it with curiosity and without judgment will shift it for you.

There are multiple ways to make money and a lot of it. Some of them are easier, less stressful and fun, while others require seriousness, dedication and hard work. Hopefully this book will encourage you to use the ones that work with ease and flow.

       To Your Best,
       Houston

How to Use This Book

This book is designed to meet you where you are, wherever you are, and help you move from there to where you want to be. It uses money and finances as the place to work and yet the principles work for any area of your life, including attitude, health, fitness or relationships as well as finances.

Reading this book now and then again six weeks from now will be like reading two different books. Simply by reading this book now will start the process of making shifts in your thinking processes that will begin making it easier to draw more money, happiness and wisdom into your life.

Use this book by reading through each and every chapter. This way you can find out the places where you may be stuck around the subject of money and having all that you want.

The chapters that resonate with you will feel good and those you can start applying more in your life. The chapters that do not resonate with you will feel not so good and those you can set aside until your curiosity draws you back to see if you can find out what those chapters were really attempting to get across to you.

This book had been infused with energy from the field (Zero Point Field) to help move you from using this book as a starting point for getting motivated and that naturally and easily transforming into your own internal inspiration. Because once you have inspiration, motivation is no longer needed.

Let me explain the difference between the two and I think you'll like it. Inspiration and motivation, the difference between Power and Force determines how hard you work to get what you really want or if you even get it at all. Have you ever heard the phrase, "That inspires me" or "that motivates me"? What is the difference and does it make a difference in whether or not you get what you want out of life?

Many people confuse the two and think they mean or represent the same thing. However, they are two different things generated in two opposite ways. Both of these trigger the power of intention inside you; however they do it in two different ways which make all the difference in the world as to the results you get and how easy or hard, fast or slow or if you even get the results you want.

Do you want to be pushed or would you like to be carried to the joyful pleasing results you are after? Do you want to have to keep artificially creating, i.e. forcing your power of intention or would you rather enjoy the pleasure of it naturally flowing from you and through you and even arranging external situations and circumstances in ways where you do less and get more accomplished?

That's the difference between the power that comes from inspiration and the force of motivation.

Inspiration…
- is self generating
- is natural
- naturally flows out of you
- requires little effort
- directs your focus
- carries you

Motivation…
- must be generated by someone other than you
- not as natural
- has to be constantly feed
- requires a lot of effort
- requires you to focus on motivation to stay motivated
- pushes you

It is a question of, "Am I going to depend on others which gives me weak personal power or am I going to look within where all my power is generated?"

Forcing something is a lot harder than having the power to let things flow, especially when you have to depend on others for the energy. Both inspiration and motivation are forms of energy that move us and can be used to get us where we want to be and to have the things we want to have.

Again the question is, "Do you want to be pushed or would you like to be carried to the joyful pleasing results you are after?" The choice is always yours now that you know there is a difference.

Presuppositions

Everything is energy (light and information)

Potential or kinetic (possibility or moving light and information)

Once kinetic energy moves it moves between energy polarities

Kinetic energy (light and information) either is moving or blocked

Energy has charge

Charge can move energy (unhook-flow) or charge can hold energy (hook-block)

All Vibrational frequencies can occupy the same space and time.

Everything can be explained from an energy (light and information) POV.

Everything operates from the principle of energy moving between energy polarities.

Thinking is the process of energy moving between two polarities… Question-Answer

The way the energy feels as an answer is determined by the quality of the question and the spin (direction)

that is applied in the asking of the question.

What generates spin…

Thinking is a form of energy comparison and at the foundational level an energy measurement. We measure things in two ways.

1. Judgments (a hard –permanent measurement)
2. Calibrations (a soft – temporary measurement)

The difference between these two energy measurements is the fundamental difference that makes the difference in accomplishing, achieving or not what one wants.

Calibrations allow for adjustments and judgments do not.

Calibrations are regarding where one is going and judgments are about where one has been.

Judgments measure the future based on the past and calibrations measure the future based on where you are and where you want to go or be. A nice thing to remember about Judgments is the legal advice giving in regards to investing in the stock market, "Past performance is no guarantee of future expectations." In other words using the past to determine the future is risky.

Judgment energy is created by making a decision of defeat. It takes a specific calibration situation; personalizes it and generalizes that one calibration incident to other calibration situations that are not similar but are perceived as similar.

Judgments are useful for things that are repetitive opening doors, sitting on chairs, putting gas in the car, etc. They are less than useful in situations with other variables such as the energy of other people and situations are a part of the mix.

Types of energy spin (direction) that can be applied to questions and statements

1. Curiosity, wonder
2. Doubt
3. Contempt-Ridicule-Disbelief Not really asking the question as the answer is already obtained.

Memories are energy held in place by four energy categories or energy post.

Category	*Energy Post*
Picture/Image	Visual pole
Body Sensation - feeling	Kinesthetic pole
Emotion – body sensation with a meaning attached	Emotional pole
Thought – (different from thinking) 1st line of the paragraph.	Auditory pole

Table 1

To change situations or circumstances (dis-create and

recreate) these four polarities have to disappear.

The major element that holds these four elements in place is Judgment. Judgment is charged energy (light and information) that hooks the individual (a vibrational energy being).

Energetically the light and information we label as judgment can be shifted or replaced by an energyvvibration that moves us and yet it does not hook us, that energy is called calibration.

Major, Major Understanding…

Every thought, action, word or deed is taken from the underlying frame of reference that *the end results will be…I (the individual) will 'feel better'. Simply everything we do, we do because we believe we will feel better because of it.*

Kinetic Energy is either flowing in the direction of the polarity one wants or it is disrupted (constricted, restricted or blocked) from flowing in the direction one wants and flows in the direction of a polarity one does not want. (The disruption caused by constrictions, restrictions and blocks, can also be called resistance.)

When energy is flowing toward its' intended polarity it feels good, when it is disrupted it does not feel good.

What causes energy to flow?

Attention IS Focus of Awareness

Energy flows, builds, strengthens and charges where attention goes. (The 2nd Forgotten Fundamental of Creation)

Side note: Keep looking for the 1st Forgotten Fundamental of Creation (it's in this book)

Everything that is physically manifested is a result of the above statement. The introduction of resistance (disruption) is the variable in how quickly or how long it takes to physically change or shift something in the physical material world.

Other terms used to describe energy flowing toward the polarity wanted or resisted and flowing toward an unwanted polarity.

- Aligned/Misaligned
- Ease/Dis ease
- Useful/Less Useful
- Calibrate/Judge
- Correct/Incorrect
- Neutral/Charged
- Stable/Unstable

The BS Factor About Money

I'm in a marketing coaching program that discusses both the external (what to do) and the internal (how to think and feel) of marketing. The other night the main coach who is very good at the external and has a better than average understanding of the inner game was talking about working on adjusting his "wealth thermostat". In other words how one can make themselves comfortable with lots of money so as not to self destruct in some fashion as a result of producing or making way more money than one usually expects or even desires.

Part of me was grateful that whether my teacher knew it or not the very act of considering what it would mean to have way more than enough money had already put him on the path of being able to handle larger and larger amounts of money coming into his experience.

Also, even though he had not yet broken through to where he could handle more and more money or more and more wealth it confirmed to me that I had done a very good thing in asking him to be one of my co-authors in this book about 'inner game', money and financial enlightenment.

One of the wonderful things about these calls is that people share what's really going on in their lives. They feel comfortable enough to say what they actually believe about things, and there are quite a few teaching moments. The level of expertise and ability runs the whole spectrum from not knowing anything to knowing more than enough to make a very comfortable living.

Here was a man who makes a very, very comfortable living, let's say 6 to 7 figures per year and his friend and mentor had challenged him about his "wealth thermostat" because they are about to release a product that will more than likely double his very, very comfortable 6 to 7 figure living. (That's what working on the Internet can do for you.) His friend has already taken steps to where his "wealth thermostat" is pretty high.

This all start by my coach telling his friend that for some reason when his friend, Joe talked about his plans to buy a Jet, it bothered him. That is what triggered the whole look into where your thermostat is set so that it doesn't sabotage your success.

So my coach has been considering where he has hang ups (limiting beliefs) about having a bunch and I mean a bunch of money. Just considering and wondering about it in this fashion does a great deal to help make the shifts so that when the money does show up he will be able to handle the amount without sabotaging himself like people who win the lottery and 3 years later they are flat broke.

I admire my coach for not only doing this but also for bring it up to everyone on the coaching call. It created a lot of discussion and I believe it was useful and helpful for many.

Now a lot of people, who are into the relationship building side of Internet marketing (there is a strictly numbers approach to Internet marketing as well), have some idea about 'inner game'. And I was reminded once again of what I call our BS Factor. BS stands for Belief System. Like my Grampa Vetter would say, "Whether you call it belief and they call it BS or vis-a-versa, it's all still BS."

Some folks were giving testimonials and encouraging others to tithe money to something whether it be church or a favorite charity or to the needy. Of course there are many people who believe this principle works regardless of the countless example of where it doesn't work. And of course they have reasons why it doesn't work and what needs to be done so it does work. Doing something external (tithing, etc) is only an indicator of what may or may not be going on internally depending on if it is coming from motivation or inspiration.

Others talked about taking action and some refined that to taking 'inspired' action. So I brought up the concept that inspiration does not require action to be taken. In fact action naturally happens when inspiration is present, there is no sense of taking action, it simply happens automatically. And the action that is taken from inspiration has zero resistance to it.

On the other hand what many confuse for inspiration is motivation. Now motivation DOES require action to be taken. Motivation requires more motivation where, inspiration requires no more inspiration. Motivation pushes you, where inspiration carries you. The way you know inspiration from motivation is you don't think about the inspiration it acts through you. Motivation is something that you think about.

In the terms I use, motivation is a Head Space activity and inspiration is a Heart Space activity. Neither one is good or bad. One is easier, faster and smoother and you do way less work though.

And even on a deeper level than that, one person said they were having to change a whole lifetime of BS-Belief System. So I asked another question. What would happen if you redefined money? And they said that's what they had been doing. What amazes me is how long most people take to change their BS-Belief System when it can be extremely easy to do and I know of at least 3 to 4 ways to do it anywhere from 10 minutes to about 4 hours.

When I realized that he was attempting to redefine his relationship to money, which is very different from redefining money itself and it takes a lot longer. I asked, what different ways are you aware of to remove the charge (energy charge) you hold around money? That question was also not understood, I asked what would happen if you thought of money as yourself? The coach replied "I'd be confused," before anyone else said anything.

The deepest lesson in all this that we didn't get to on the training call is it all boils down to *money isn't real*. We think it is but it isn't. It is our BS-Belief System that makes something that has no inherent meaning have a meaning that creates a charge that causes us to separate it out as something apart from us.

Money just like everything else people, places and things are simply us in another form. OR as one teacher put it, "It is you and you are your creation. So both you (who you think you are) and it (money, others, places and things) are only what you create it to be. Because of the 1st Forgotten Fundamental of Creation, "The Individual Is The Meaning Maker", we give the meaning that something is separate and more important than self.

Now the interesting thing about all this is it doesn't matter which level you choose to play on. In other words how clear you are on 'inner game' (some clarity helps and the more you have the more it helps) there are ways right now to make money on the Internet.

Even if you don't understand that 'inner game' is the only game there is, you can still make money. Probably enough to live comfortably on and yes there are programs out there that will help you clear up your life (your BS-Belief System) enough that you can be more successful and more comfortable than you are right now. So go find some training and make the changes so you can be happier, healthier, wealthier and wiser.

Over the years I've offered multiple books, programs

and trainings on "Inner Game, The Only Game There Is" and the end results are people make more money, have better relationships, and healthier heath as a side effect of mastering the Inner Game. We are always developing new tools and techniques.

We have separate tools you can use such as HeartSpace™ (www.beyondclearing.com) that has three levels.

Level 1 is the fastest stress reliever process in the world.

Level 2 sets it up so that business and personal relationships work with ease and flow.

Level 3 is the fastest way to glimpse an experience of spiritual enlightenment.

A favorite of many is This One Secret (www.thisonesecret.com)that uses spin in the best way to get what you want.

One of the first tools we developed was Secret Success (www.secretsuccess.com) our ecoaching program.

Or we can help you with more direct one-on-one approach in a mentoring program (www.docresults.com) to get what it is you want to get. I am in the process of developing a 12 week program called "The Habit Of Freedom – Off The Hook Enlightenment" which is probably the best course I've every constructed. And as with everything in duality (where we live) there is two sides to freedom, freedom from and freedom to and your wealth depends on it.

The Money Rant And More BS Factor

Most people are aware that each person's reality is not the same. Even though we mentally acknowledge that everyone is usually entitled to their version of reality we often, feel that our reality is better than some peoples and there might be a few people who have better realities than we do.

What 99.9% of people believe is that their reality is what is real and in one sense that is true. Your individual reality is 100% true for you because of one thing and one thing only. You BSed yourself into believing it, BS stands for Belief System. Another thing that most do not realize is, truth and accuracy, are not the same thing. Your individual reality is 100% true for you and yet it is not accurate. Accurate in terms of getting you the results you say you want.

What most people are not aware of is that there is a big difference between reality and actuality. Actuality is external, outside of you and Reality is an inside job. People have not yet come to the realization that 'reality' is created between the left one and the right one, i.e. the left ear and the right ear.

The biggest secret in the world is that "Reality is BS", and it has already been said "BS stands for Belief System". Every one of us is constantly spouting BS-Belief System and the only time we call someone on their BS (or get called on ours) is when it runs contrary to our own BS-Belief System, which means most of the time we are agreeing and supporting the BS of each other, which takes us away from actuality and what really works.

This is how 'Consensus Reality' is created. It's not actually true, correct or accurate we only act as if it is. Consensus Reality is what most people agree is true, correct and accurate. However, it is far from accurate, not very correct as it leaves have's and have's not; those who have stuff and those who do not have stuff and in this discussion those who have money and those who don't. And it is true only because we've used energy to make it apparent reality.

The reason reality is only BS-Belief System is because of the 1st Forgotten Fundamental of Creation; "The Individual IS the Meaning Maker". Without someone to apply meaning nothing has any inherent meaning. As one master teacher used to say, "You don't have to believe anything *but whatever you do believe* **'will become'** your perceived and felt reality." In other words nothing has any meaning until you or I add it.

The best example of the 1st Forgotten Fundamental is a child. You have to repeat instructions over and over and over to a child until the moment that they add meaning for themselves (and usually it is the meaning you have added) and once they add meaning you no longer have to give the same instructions. Once a child adds meaning for themselves we no longer have to tell them to play in the yard and not in the street or , eat with a fork and not your hands or chew with your mouth closed and if you are from the south say "yes mama, no mama; thank you and please".

The reason that BS-Belief Systems are so strong is the 2nd Forgotten Fundamental of Creation; "Energy flows, builds, strengthens and charges where attention goes."

No matter what your belief system is, Liberal, Conservative, Christian, Muslim, Jewish, Atheist, etc. there are at a minimum 3 problems that haunt one's BS-Belief system. These problems keep you stuck and limit your potential to be, do or have what you really want in life.

The first problem that trips up our belief system is an unquestioned accepted belief, that my belief is right. The problem is that at the time the belief moved from a thought form to where it became a belief, it was right in that instance and at that time. If we believe our belief is right when someone disagrees with our belief we take it personally and our feelings get hurt and we lash out at others.

However, location and time are two things that cause beliefs (which are a particular form of judgment) to be less than useful and often inaccurate. You see a belief depends on the past to predict the future and as the stock market has often told us, "Past performance is no guarantee of future results." And yet, since we believe our beliefs are correct and right we unwittingly carry them through time which stretches the accuracy because the bull's-eye is not that spread out.

The second insidious belief about our belief is that our beliefs are not to be questioned. If something is right, there is no need to examine it, right? And unfortunately for us, an unexamined belief is one of the biggest road blocks on the road to success and financial enlightenment. Have you ever been amazed that out of the millions and millions of bytes of information we receive every second we can delete, distort and generalize all that information down to a 'once and for all', 'this is it, 'this is how it must be forever' thing we call a belief?

And the third problem with our BS-Belief System is we use it as our reason to no longer think. As my Grampa Vetter would say, "A belief (conclusion) is where we decided to stop thinking." And probably worst than stopping our thinking, a belief STOPS our intuition. Our intuition is where our innovation comes from. Intuition is where our inspiration comes from and our BS-Belief System because it is based on judgments, curtails our access to our intuition.

Because of these 3 hindrances to our success they create another problem and that is one of the main reasons for developing beliefs in the first place. It was the belief that having these beliefs will make me happy. So because of that it takes us back to the first problem, we have equated being right with being happy. How many people (including you) defend and argue about and for what we know to be "right", believing if everyone else would see it my way, we'd all be happy. That is the consequences of the 3 problems that haunt our BS-Belief System. And like my Grampa Vetter used to say, "It seems you'd rather be right than happy, right?"

Now Concerning money…

Consensus Reality (BS-Belief System) says: (or something similar)

- Money is real
- Money is evil
- Money is separate from you
- If you have a lot of money you are greedy
- Give (tithe) 10% to make money flow
- Work hard to earn money
- Save money for a rainy day
- Money is the root of all evil

Actuality is:

Money Isn't Real it is ALL Your Creation
&
Money isn't the only thing that isn't real.

Differences between Reality and Actuality...

Consensus (Your) Reality: You are a separate individual and there are things that are more powerful than you and things that are less powerful than you.

Actuality: You are the Power and Presence of Divinity

Consensus (Your) Reality: You are separate from that which is called God (Source, The Universe, etc)

Actuality: You are Divinity Extended

Consensus (Your) Reality: You have a certain amount of abundance/lack, power/weakness, peace/pain, joy/sadness

Actuality: You are infinite abundance, power, peace and joy

Consensus (Your) Reality: Some things you have control over and a lot of things you don't have any control over, things happen to you

Actuality: You as the leading Edge Extension of Divinity are pure positive energy creating everything. No one can create for you or in your experience, only you. (No one can think or feel for you) All the power is in you and Your Extended self and how you use the field.

Consensus (Your) Reality: There is you and there are separate people, places and things

Actuality: You are the only one here. Everything and everyone else is your creation following the script you wrote for them exactly.

Actuality: You and your Inner Being are Source Energy and Source is the powerful Stream of Consciousness

Actuality: You are abundant and when you accept that (in your thoughts and feelings) it shows in your experience.

Actuality: Everything is Energy and works by vibrational relativity.

Actuality: Set your intent and pop it into your hologram, Take the power out of the bubbles (realities) you have created.

Actuality: Focus on what you want and not on what you don't want to manifest your desires.

Choosing Your Own Target

Pat O'Bryan

I've noticed that people need someone to look up to and someone to look down on. It's unfortunate. But, how do you know how you're doing if you don't compare yourself to… something or someone?

Recently, I got a lesson in letting go of these comparisons. It changed my life in a good way. Read on-

The upstairs porch at Brewsters Pizza is one of the most delightful places on the planet. An elevated, shaded area with room for maybe thirty-fifty people to stand, or maybe twenty to sit comfortably. There are tables and big, comfy chairs.

The view is stunning. To the left is the road to Devil's Backbone, straight ahead you're looking over the Wimberley valley. Hills, trees, and spectacular sunsets stretch out as far as the eye can see. The hills slope down to the Blanco River, which isn't really visible from the porch, but you can tell where it is.

The audio can be distracting. In addition to the sounds one would expect in an upscale pizza restaurant your peaceful reverie can be broken by Harleys and sports cars blatting down the hill- all of which would benefit from mufflers, in my opinion.

Recently, Dr. Joe Vitale and I had a late lunch on that porch. I'd been out of town for a month, visiting my off-the-grid cabin in Terlingua. In addition to being buddies, Joe and I are business partners so we get together every now and then to catch up on what we've been doing and to plan future adventures. Joe's fascinated by my stories of Terlingua. He says, "it's not just another world, it's another planet."

I won't bore you with the personal stuff, although I will share just one… while I was in Terlingua, my 56th birthday came and went. Joe surprised me with a present- an Erlewine travel guitar, and not just any Erlewine travel guitar. This one was one of the ones that Mark Erlewine made himself in collaboration with ZZ Top's Billy Gibbons. It's a little jewel, precision designed and crafted out of natural wood. It looks like a toy, but is in fact a serious rock and roll implement of pleasure. I was delighted, and it now is displayed prominently along with the rest of my guitar collection.

So, let me set the stage. I'm sitting at a table on the elevated porch looking out over the hill country. Joe is to my right. In front of us are a couple of Vitale steaks, with trimmings. (Brewster's is a pizza joint, and one of the best in the galaxy. There are some off-menu items that Bruce can be persuaded to fix if you give him some lead time. The Vitale steak is one of those. It ain't a cheap thing, but it is possibly the best steak money can buy. Anywhere.)

Very nice cigars and very old scotch round out the table settings.

To my left sits Bruce Collie.

In a nutshell, I am surrounded by two of the most effective over-achievers on the planet. Joe is the author of 50+ books, a movie star, and one of the best Internet Marketers alive. Bruce is a former NFL star with two superbowl rings. He's run successful construction businesses, invests successfully in real estate, and his current restaurant/brew-pub is a smashing success. These guys know success. It's where they live.

In the middle, there's me.

Here's where the lesson happens. I'm a real good guitar player, but I'm not as good as Joe Bonamassa, Eric Clapton, Eric Johnson, etc. I used to make records, and they're also good, but not as good as The Beatles, for example.

That's always bothered me. No matter how well I did, no matter how cool my gigs were, there was always someone who was doing better. U2, for example, make more money in one night than I made in my entire music career. Thinking like that can make you wonder why you bother.

Now, I'm also an author. I've written four books, two of which were best sellers. In most gatherings of authors,

I'd feel pretty successful. However, I'm sitting with a guy who has written 50+ books, many of which were best sellers.

I'm also a pretty good Internet Marketer, and I teach Internet Marketing. However, there are Internet Marketers who make more money than I do, and in Internet Marketing, that's one of the ways we keep score. As a matter of fact, there are Internet Marketers who make as much money in a week as I do in a year. Joe's one of those.

It's kind of like being a reasonably good entertainer, and your buddy is Elvis. In the Internet Marketing world, Joe is Elvis. He's also a real nice guy. He'll listen with interest while I talk about what I'm doing. Then, he'll share what he's been up to.

Amazing promotions, trips to Russia, Poland and Chile, best-selling Nightingale Conant programs and books, private masterminds with the top minds on the planet, for example. Compared to Joe, I might as well have stayed in bed.

And then there's Bruce. I've done some interesting things, but nothing I've done compares with winning the Superbowl. In American iconography, that's about the coolest thing you CAN do. And Bruce did it twice.

After the steak, we fired up some amazing cigars, topped off our cups, and had a mini-mastermind meeting. Maybe it was the scotch that led me to bring up the subject, maybe it was the cigars, but I brought up the subject of comparison.

I told Joe and Bruce that I constantly compared myself to them and other successful people. And, in those comparisons, I didn't always come off as the uber-successful person that I wanted to. My question was, "who do you compare yourselves to?"

The answer surprised me. They both said, "I don't."

I asked for clarification. Everybody compares themselves to somebody, right?

Bruce said, "I'm only competing with me." He then went on to talk about injuries, car wrecks, pins through bones, playing football games with broken bones, and businesses that seemed to want to fail. He viewed the apparent adversity as a challenge, and used those challenges to get stronger. When a business wasn't working, he either closed it or changed it- and worked even harder to make it a success. Bottom line, he may fail, but not for long. The game ain't over till it's over, and ultimately, he's going to win.

Joe had a different take: "I look for projects that would be fun," he said. "I look for something new and interesting that I want to do, and then I do it."

I got the feeling that although Joe is very aware of what others in his industry are doing, he doesn't really look to others for inspiration. They're old news.

I also know Joe constantly asks himself the question, "what would be better than that?"

So, I suspect, based on years of observation, that he comes up with an initial idea that he thinks would be fun and profitable, and then plays the "what would be better" game with that idea.

There are people who are more successful than Bruce and Joe. The lesson for me is that they spend absolutely no time thinking about that.

That conversation took place a couple of weeks ago, and the more I reflect on it and learn the lessons from it the better I feel. Of course, the Beatles made better records than I did. However, thousands of people enjoy my music. It's OK that I wasn't as successful as they were- by a long shot. I made the best Pat O'Bryan records that I could make, and they stand on their own.

The same deal with guitar playing. Yes, when Eric Clapton closes his eyes and starts channeling a long dead blues master his playing is transcendent. At my best, I'll never be that good. And yet, I can make a blues band chug like a locomotive. I've watched the dance floor fill to capacity when I start laying down the blues. I could always be a second rate Eric Clapton, but it's more fun and healthier for me to be a first-rate Pat O'Bryan.

And then there's Internet Marketing. Music can be a matter of taste and opinion. In IM, we keep score with money.

At one point, I looked at Joe and said, "How will I ever catch _____?" (Fill in the blank with the name of a very successful Internet Marketer who I have been trying to "catch" since I started.)

Joe said, "You don't have to."

And I exhaled.

Over the next few weeks, I got it.

I'm not a better Internet Marketer because I make more money than one person, and another person isn't better than me because they make more money than I do. We're all who we are, and we're all competing with ourselves.

All I (and you) have to do is be the best we can be, and that can look a lot of different ways.

For example, I not only run one of the best Internet Marketing coaching programs in the world, I run (I think) the cheapest Internet Marketing coaching program in the world. I could, and possibly should, charge much more. But, there are other benefits to me besides money. I get to work with absolute beginners who are just starting out. By working with them, I can keep them from getting hurt- among other things. I don't do upsells to my coaching clients. I transparently show them what I do that works, what I've tried that didn't work, and help them achieve realistic goals that, over time, has brought some of them to pretty substantial success. That's success to me.

One day I was talking to Ray Wylie Hubbard, who is a pretty famous songwriter/performer and a neighbor. We've played some gigs together. We were talking about success. Ray's pretty successful, but he's not as successful as, for example, his friend Willie Nelson.

Anyway, the way Ray put is was, "everybody else is ganged up shooting at that target over there," he said, pointing to his left. "I'm shooting at this one over here," he continued, pointing to his right.

In other words, you get to define your success.

To Ray, it's not about having the hot hit single of the moment. It's about creating the next great song, and adding it to a life's work that contains a lot of great songs, a stream of interesting gigs stretching decades into the past and, hopefully, into the future.

Ray, like Joe and Bruce, is very successful. They're successful because they define what success means to them, and don't let others define them or their success.

To me, that's remarkably liberating.

You mean, it's ok for me to take the night off to watch the sun set and the stars come out? It's ok to take a day off and go for a ride through the hill country with Betsy? It's ok to write a book that I want to write, instead of one I know will sell?

The answer is a resounding "yes!"

It's not about maximizing your income. It's about maximizing your life.

Once I got that, I felt like a huge weight had lifted. I decide what target I shoot at. Nobody else gets a vote.

Try it. See how that feels.

Here's the punch line. Once I stopped comparing myself to others and just set my own course, my income just about doubled. It's only been a few weeks, but it's consistent.

Pick your own target. Define success your way. And then shoot for the bulls-eye.

You can't miss.

Pat O'Bryan is a leading Internet marketing coach and produces many Internet marketing products and 'inner games' products. He is an author and his latest bestseller is Money From Anywhere (www.moneyfromanywhere.com).

To find out more or to get into Pat's coaching program visit www.patobryan.com.

Eye of the Needle, or,
The Shocking Spiritual Truth About Money

Dr. Joe Vitale

Warning: The following may be controversial and confrontational. I'm doing my best to help you prosper during perceived tough times. I'm getting "in your face" so you can shake off limiting beliefs, drop the excuses, and begin to help yourself and others. May the following inspire you to do just that.

Often people have trouble attracting money because they unconsciously believe it's evil. You wouldn't want to attract anything you thought was evil, would you?

But is money really evil?

Ben Witherington writes in his book, *Jesus and Money*:
"Money in itself is just a means of exchange. It is no more inherently evil than any other material thing God created."

Actually, the quote about money being evil is a partial one from Paul, not Jesus. Paul wasn't enlightened but wisely warned about the love of money potentially being a problem.

I totally agree. Loving money over life itself could take you from the essence of life, not toward it. As I explained in my book, *Attract Money Now*, the wealthy people I know don't love money. They appreciate it and leverage it, but they're not in love with it. Big difference.

What about the story where Jesus said, "A rich man can't get into heaven"?

It's a misquote. Jesus said it would be difficult for a rich man to get in, not that he "can't" get in.

And why difficult?

It's difficult to get through the eye of a needle when you're carrying a lot of stuff.

As I've taught, it's fine to have material things — the material is the concrete form of the spiritual — it's just not so fine to be attached to them. If your happiness is dependent on them, then you're missing the miracle of this very moment.

What really matters is what is in your heart concerning money. If it's your be-all and end-all, then money is your God and that, from a Jesus/Paul viewpoint, is a no-no. But if money is neutral to you, just a means to an end, then you are probably pure in heart concerning it. Godspeed to you.

What I do is appreciate money and use it to express my inspirations and Divinity. Money is just a cool agreed-upon tool to get things done. With it I can help myself, family and friends, and distribute it to causes and people

I believe in. I do all that and more. It's about being at peace with money.

I love Arnold Patent's quote, in his book, *Money*:

The sole purpose of money is to express appreciation.

When you realize that money is neutral, that you can use it with a heart full of love, and you can be a steward for it to see that the Divine is expressed through you, then you are clear to attract all the money you will allow.

Mother Teresa said –

"Money will come if we seek first the Kingdom of God – the rest will be given."

What is this "Kingdom of God"?

Religious wars have been fought over the answers. For me, it's following your Divine connection; the voice in your heart that whispers what It wants you to do next. When you follow It, you move in the direction of experiencing and creating this Kingdom right here, right now.

What's worth remembering is you can't tell what is Divinely guided in another person any more than they can tell what is Divinely guided within you.

Jay Leno and his car collection might be Divinely guided. I can't honestly say. Neither can you.

Bill Gates and his fortune might be there because he followed Divine guidance. We have no way of knowing.

Jimmie Vaughan has 200 guitars. Not inspired collecting? How would you know?

Donald Trump might be following his own spiritual path. Who's to say, unless you project your own idea of wealth and spirituality onto him, and then who's to say you're right?

You're on an ego trip if you feel you can determine someone's motivation. We have to focus on our own connection and actions and refrain from judgments.

Scot Anderson, in his book, *God Wants You Rich*, says -

> *"What did Jesus say when someone was dumping perfume on His feet that was worth one year's salary — in today's numbers more than $40,000 — and someone said it should be given to the poor? Jesus said, 'The poor you will have with you always'."*

Anderson goes on to say, *"…Get out of your holier-than-thou attitude. Stop judging others and live your own life."*

That may sound harsh, but maybe it's time to be more direct.

Buddha had his own thoughts on money, of course. According to *The Buddha's Teachings on Prosperity: At Home, At Work, in the World* by Bhikkhu Basnagoda Rahula –

> *"The Buddha never imposed limitations on his lay follower's efforts to be successful; instead, he clearly encouraged them to strive for success. Whether in "trading, cattle farming, archery, government service, or any other profession or industry," a layperson should strive to advance in his or her respective field. Notably, the motivation to achieve success is an important requirement in any person's life — an attitude of "I*

have a job that's enough for me to live on" has no place in the Buddha's teaching.

Next, the Buddha set no limits to a layperson's wealth and never told his prosperous lay followers to stop or slow down. Instead, he unequivocally encouraged them to plan, organize, and even to obtain more..."

Buddha encouraged attracting more?

Jesus didn't think money was evil?

The sole purpose of money is to express appreciation?

Pretty eye-opening, isn't it?

Given these insights, how do you feel about money now?

Whether you think money is spiritual or not doesn't matter when you need it in today's world to survive and thrive. You best make peace with it. If you want to help yourself and others, you best clean up your attitude toward wealth.

But how?

Attract Money for Good

I've created entire books and courses to help you get clear and then attract money to use for your own Divinely guided actions. Some of them, such as *Attract Money Now* (www.attractmoneynow.com), are free.

Have you read the book? If not, why not? If so, did you apply the seven steps in it? If not, why not?

Too many people have shrugged off the pursuit of money saying it was evil or material, or that Jesus or Buddha wouldn't use or acquire or accumulate money today.

Come on. Obviously, that's not true. They wouldn't

be attached to money, but they'd certainly attract it and leverage it for good.

And who's good would they use it for?

Their choice.

Meaning they wouldn't listen to you, but to their own inner direction. You might not even agree with how they handled their wealth. You might even be surprised and confused by it. You might even think they were greedy.

Do you think your opinion would stop them?

Hardly.

They'd adapt to modern times, too.

Do you really think they'd ride in an ox cart today? Not fly in an airplane to get overseas? Not have a bank account — or entrust someone to have one for them? Not do marketing to get the word out?

When I wrote my dissertation to earn one of my doctorate degrees, it was on the marketing methods every great religion and metaphysical movement did to attract followers. They all used money and marketing to spread the good word of their ideas. All of them.

Apparently their leaders were just fine with money.

But let's dig below the surface of all this:

Why do you even care what anyone does with their money? Or what Buddha or Jesus thought about wealth?

Sometimes people use not having money as an excuse for not following inspirations.

I'm sorry, but excuses are no longer allowed.

It's time to awaken.

You have a job to do here. I don't know what it is.

You do.

Dr. Kalinda Rose Stevenson, in her very enlightening e-book, *Going Broke With Jesus*, says –

"When you have money, you have the power to have a greater impact in the world. Most of us are used to playing small roles, partly because we don't have enough money."

John Kay, in his book, *Obliquity*, pointed out that the wealthiest people – from Andrew Carnegie to Bill Gates – achieved their riches through a passion for their work, not because they set materialistic goals.

Passion.

That's the real ticket to success and the real thing to focus on.

Don't let lack of money or time or energy or experience or education stop you. Far too many people with less than you have created their dreams.

Focus on your passion.

Don't let opinions about what Jesus or Buddha would think or do stop you from following your own inspirations. That's a cop-out.

Focus on your passion.

Don't let religious bullies or well-meaning interpreters of ancient spiritual literature distort your perception of the world and what's possible for you.

Focus on your passion.

It's time to act.

Will you?

Let me be even more in your face: Stop judging people with money and how they use it. How does that serve you, except to make you feel self-righteous? Start attracting money and using it for the good you see will help the most. If you want to make a difference, make a difference. It begins with you. Will you sit on the sidelines and judge or will you enter the game and be part of the solution? Will you follow your passion or not? The whistle has blown. The game is on. The clock is ticking. Get on the field and play. Now.

The Inside Scoop!
Subjectivity Inside Objectivity for Business

John La Valle

So you think you know what's going on inside? Do you believe you make the best decisions possible? Each and every moment of each and every day, you and I are thinking thoughts, some are obvious, that is conscious, and most are not, that is, unconscious.

What most people have never been trained to do is to uncover how they think, or how they can become aware of how they think, or even how to change the ways in which they think. And as soon as we become aware of how we think, there opens the doorway to possibilities, whether it be in business or other times and places.

As business leaders, we want to believe we are making decisions on objectivity, and so they are, to us, logical, irrefutable. But when you look inside the "objectivity" at the subjectivity factor, soon you realize where the fallacies lie which can always support any decision, and can therefore be changed, argued, rediscovered, supported, etc. This is because our complex, not easily understood, brains operate on what could be described as hard science, and yet, are so subjective that we are often "misunderstood" by others.

Let's conduct a short "objective" experiment here with something you believe to be "objective" for you. The risk here is when you think something is "objective", when it may not be. Let's first look at one of dictionary.com's definition of "objective" so we understand what criteria to use for this:

> 5. *not influenced by personal feelings, interpretations, or prejudice; based on facts; unbiased: an objective opinion.*

This alone presents one of the challenges: "not influenced by personal feelings"! How can someone do that "rationally"? Now here's one worth considering: "based on facts". *How do we know these facts to be "true"? Do we gather enough information until we "feel" it's right? Until we are "satisfied"?*

Let's dive into something many people don't make distinctions about: What is on the outside of your head, and what's going on in the inside? And do you know the difference? Many people do not. So, let's, for the experiment's sake, say that facts occur on the outside, and these are things we can "see, hear, feel (tactile sensation, as in touch)" Without making the argument here about "do we see what we think we see?" Or "hear what we think we hear"? (Notice the word "think", which then requires our internal processing, which takes us from the outside of our head). Let's assume that we agree on what we both see on the outside, so this agreement would be considered "objective" by both of us, (and also known as "shared reality").

But if we take a look on the inside and determine "how" each of us represents this internally, the chances are that we would both represent it differently. How, you may ask? Easily: Years ago, Dr. Richard Bandler, co-creator of Neuro-Linguistic Programming identified in his book *Using Your Brain For a Change* sub parts of our sensory modalities, which are visual, auditory, kinesthetic, olfactory and gustatory. Each of these sub parts, called submodalities, are further distinctions of the three major modalities, for example:

Visual would include, but not limited to: movies vs. slides, black and white vs. color, bright vs. dim, distance, size of the image, etc.

Auditory would include, but not limited to: volume, tone, pitch, tempo, stereo vs. one ear, distance, angle, etc.

Kinesthetic would include, but not limited to: location in body, pressure, temperature, movement, etc.

Now on to our experiment: Now think of something "objective" for you. Let's make it easy: you are looking at this text. This is easy. As you are looking at it, you are processing the data inside your brain. Is the information clear? Is it clear on the outside? They are just characters on a page. Is it clear on the inside? Hmmmm.... What's the difference between the inside and the outside? When you use some of the above submodalities to discern the differences, what are they? List them for yourself.

Let's conduct a different experiment: Think of something "objective" for you. Your car, if you have one. If not, something like that. You "know" your car. You also "like" or "dislike" your car. So this has a "feeling" attached to it. How much do you like your car? This is difficult to ascertain in objective terms. Notice how far away the image is and how big the image is. Move it further away and make the image smaller. Do you like it as much, or more, or less? Notice the differences in submodalities. Then put it back the way it was in your mind.

We can conduct more experiments with sounds, feelings, etc. The point here is that while we think we make decisions "objectively" we really don't because there are many variables that are, in fact, subjective. This is what we refer to as our "gut instinct."

Now, the same applies to using your "spiritualness" and/or "mental capabilities" to bring forth "physicalness". There is one extremely important and very valuable component when thinking on the inside how to manifest on the outside. Having worked with and trained thousands of people through the years, the critical factor is this: Make fine distinctions in your thinking. And it's just not enough to want that "Testosterossa" (as I call it). That is simply the reward for "doing" certain behaviors. It is the behaviors that are critical for your thinking internally. When setting goals, objectives or making decisions, think of the behaviors you want to be able to do. The behaviors are what generate the results. Period.

And with all the subtle subjective variables available (submodalities), make whatever adjustments necessary so that you generate those behaviors.

The inside generates what is possible on the outside. Then from the outside you can calibrate the differences between what result you are actually getting and what result you wanted and make other adjustments as necessary to get the behaviors you want for yourself. This really opens the possibilities. They are up to you, after all.

Now Go For It!

John J. La Valle is a Licensed Master Trainer of NLP™ (www.NeuroLinguisticProgramming.com) *& DHE™** (www.DesignHimanEngineering.com), *who has been in the training & development field for almost twenty-five years and who has brought NLP™ and DHE™ into the business arena for the past almost 25 years. He is the co-author, with Richard Bandler, of Persuasion Engineering®* (www.PersuasionEngineering.com).

John is also a member of The Society of Neuro-Linguistic Programming™ (www.purenlp.com/society.html), *The American Society of Training & Development, and is certified with The National Values Center. In addition to Practitioner & Master Practitioner programs,* (www.purenlp.com/nlpsgsch.html) *John specializes in Sales & Influence, manufacturing applications, team building, management and leadership skills, and Design*

Human Engineering™*. His extensive background in socio-technical systems design, employee involvement and participative management systems has earned him a reputation for getting results in many Fortune 100 companies.

His training style enables him to get right to core of the issues, where he well known for his ability to take seemingly complex issues and breaking them down into easily solvable opportunities for organizations.

John publishes John's HOT NLP TIPS NEWSLETTER (www.nlp-newsletter.com) *monthly.*

How You Can Eliminate Beliefs For Good

Morty Lefkoe

Most of the techniques that proclaim to permanently eliminate long-held beliefs don't work. Why? And what do the successful techniques do that make them successful?

In order to understand precisely what it takes to get rid of beliefs, you need to understand how we form beliefs.

Because our survival as human beings is always at stake (even though our spiritual being is eternal), we have a built in survival mechanism that has us constantly asking about everything we encounter: Good for me or bad for me? Conducive to my survival or inimical to my survival? In other words, we are constantly appraising everything we come in contact with and asking (unconsciously): What does this mean?

As children we want to know why mom and dad (on whom our lives depend) are angry with us, or why they aren't around when we want them, or why we can never seem to please them. For most kids between the ages of two and six, the answers to these three questions usually are: Mistakes and failure are bad. I'm not important. I'm not good enough.

Here's how the beliefs are formed

After asking ourselves: What do these events mean?—we then "make up" one possible meaning. And then we "attribute" that meaning to the events, after which it seems as if the meaning is inherent in the events. In other words, it then seems to us as if we discovered the meaning in the events.

Because the overwhelming majority of people are "visual"—in other words, they know reality based on what they can "see"—they know their beliefs are true because they think they can see them in the world. Once you think you can see something, logic will never talk you out of what you think you have seen "out there."

Let's apply what I've just explained about how beliefs are formed to the most common belief people have, I'm not good enough. Mom and dad want quiet. Young kids are rarely quiet. Mom and dad want the house to be neat. Kids are rarely neat. Mom and dad want to serve dinner when it's ready and leave the house when they are ready to leave the house. Kids are busy playing and doing what they want to do; mealtime and leaving the house are not always a priority for them. As a result, many times each day children do not live up to their parents' expectations.

At best parents respond with annoyance and frustration, expressed in facial expressions, a tone of voice, and comments like: "What's wrong with you?" "How many times do I have to tell you?" "Don't you ever listen?" (At worst, parents use physical abuse and other punishments.)

When a child asks herself, what does it mean that she is not doing what her parents want repeatedly and what do her parents' responses mean, the answer 99% of all children give is: I'm not good enough. (My associates and I have talked to well over 13,000 clients who have told us this.)

If she actually were not good enough, her parents' responses to her behavior would make sense. In other words, this belief is a reasonable interpretation of mom and dad's response to her when she is a very young child.

Here is the important part: Once she gives this meaning to the events, it seems to her as if her meaning (her belief) is inherent in the events—as if when she looks at the events she is discovering the meaning "out there" in the world. Once that happens, her belief about the way the world is becomes an entrenched "fact."

Most of the techniques designed to get rid of beliefs never deal with how the belief got formed and what a belief actually is: A statement about reality that it seems you saw in reality. And because you think you saw your beliefs, you will hold on to them—despite understanding logically that the belief isn't true and despite understanding that it is self-defeating to continue to hold on to the belief. It is virtually impossible to not believe something you think you "saw."

How to get rid of the belief

So how can you eliminate the belief quickly, easily, and permanently? Here are the simple steps.

Take a look at a given belief and realize it is one "valid" interpretation of your experiences. And then realize that there are other possible interpretations that hadn't occurred to you at the time you formed the belief, but, nevertheless, could just as easily account for the events. At which point you realize your belief is "a truth" and not "the truth."

Then the crucial part comes: Put yourself back into the events that led to the belief and, as you look at them, ask yourself: Doesn't it seem as if I can "see" [the belief]? The answer for visual people will always be: "Yes. And you would have seen it too if you had been there."

Then ask yourself: Did I really "see" it? Because if you really saw it, you would be able to describe it: color, shape, location, etc. When you realize that you can't describe it, you immediately realize that, in fact, you never really "saw" the belief. You only saw events, but the meaning of the events—in other works, the beliefs you formed about the events—existed only in your mind.

At this point, for most visual people, the belief is gone. It existed and resisted being extinguished because you thought you had seen it. As soon as you realize you never saw it, that it existed only in your mind, it is no longer something you thought you discovered and saw in the world; it is only one interpretation of many possible interpretations that has existed only in your mind.

As the final clincher, ask yourself if the events that led to the formation of the belief have any inherent meaning. Did they have any meaning before you give them a meaning? By that I mean, can you draw any conclusion for sure from these events? You will quickly realize that the events that led to your belief have many different possible meanings; there is no one meaning that is inherently true. So, while the events might have had consequences at the time they happened, they have no inherent meaning. Any meaning exists only in your mind, not in the world.

At that point, for predominantly visual people, the belief is permanently gone.

Emotionally kinesthetic people are slightly different

The scenario is slightly different for those people who are not visual, who are primarily emotionally kinesthetic. If you are one of these people, you don't know reality primarily based on what you see, but based on what you feel. If you feel something a lot, it must be true. Why would you be having a feeling over and over if there weren't something in the world causing it?

These people—when asked: Didn't it seem as if you saw [your belief]?—answer: "I don't know what you mean by seeing it; I felt it."

Here's how to get rid of a belief if this describes how

you function. Ask yourself if the events that caused the belief made you feel [the words of the belief]. The answer will be, yes

Then remind yourself that you had said earlier that the events had no inherent meaning and ask yourself: Is it possible for events that have no inherent meaning to make you feel anything? The answer, of course, is no. So if the events that seemed to have caused the feeling didn't cause the feeling, what did?

The answer is simple: the meaning you had previously given the events. In other words, the feeling is the result of the belief you had formed. If you had given the events a different meaning, that different meaning would have produced a different feeling. The way to prove this is to imagine the earlier events, observing them as a participant, and then giving the events one of the alternative interpretations you had given the events earlier in the process.

When you do that the "feeling of the belief" is gone.

It becomes clear that having the feeling of the belief repeatedly tells you nothing about the validity of the feeling, because the feeling was not caused by events in the world. It was caused totally by you, by the meaning you already had given the events.

When you say the words of the belief at that point, they will sound meaningless and silly. The belief will be gone.

To summarize: Beliefs are statements about reality that we feel are the truth, that are facts about the world.

We are convinced our beliefs are true because we think we saw them in the world and because we felt them so often that they must be true (or else why would we have felt them so often?). Once we realize we never saw the beliefs in the world, that they were only in our mind, and that the feelings we had repeatedly were only because of meanings we gave meaningless events—the beliefs will be gone forever.

Getting rid of beliefs quickly, easily, and permanently is actually very easy when you understand how beliefs are formed and what it takes to eliminate a belief. And now you understand that.

We are in the process of creating an on-line training where you can become proficient in each of the steps of the Lefkoe Belief Process for eliminating beliefs. If you are interested in receiving advance notification, please let me know.

If you haven't yet eliminated at least one of your limiting self-esteem beliefs using the Lefkoe Belief Process, go to www.recreateyourlife.com/free where you can eliminate one negative belief free.

For information about eliminating 23 of the most common limiting beliefs and conditionings, which cause eight of the most common problems in our lives, please check out www.recreateyourlife.com.

How Much is that Doggie in the Window?
The Myth of Money

Jerry Stocking

Is money or is a dog man's best friend?

I suggest that neither, the trusty canine or the filthy lucre is man's best friend.

It seems clear to me that what is man's best friend is still a mystery to us. I think I know what man's best friend is, but it will take a bit of explaining to get around to it. In just a little bit I will tell you specifically what man's best friend is. First, let's explore the hidden secrets of the doggie in the window and money.

The secret of the doggie in the window is that the doggie got a clue and just needs attention. It can't really think much. It is as content, or discontent, as it can be just lying around and getting petted every once in a while. The doggie won't judge his master, not because he loves the master but because he hasn't the ability to judge at all. The master effortlessly and invisibly projects the best of him or herself onto the unwitting hound thinking all the while that the dog holds its owner in high esteem. It not only doesn't hold the master in high esteem, it doesn't hold anything at all. Rover's empty eyes provide sweet relief from all the judgments, thoughts, and beliefs, worries, to do lists, goals and desires of the master. The dog offers nothing which is welcome relief from all the promising something's the master is busy chasing. (Fetching)

The doggie reflects the best of us back to us and in return we call him man's best friend.

You don't spend an extended time with the dog though. You have to go to work, of course. How much time you spend at work reveals that you really don't prefer the dog.

You prefer the pursuit of money to the dog. Money is more than willing to direct an inordinate amount of what you do, while still letting you refer to your dog as man's best friend. Money dominates much of your time and attention.

How much of your life has been about the accumulation or just plain thinking about money? How often do you use the absence of money as an excuse for not doing something? Money is secretly man's best friend. But unlike the dog which is always man's best friend, waiting tail wagging at the door, money is also man's worst enemy.

Money drives you crazy. You use money as an excuse for all sorts of things. You do or don't do things all for the sake of money.

What is money? Most money is paper with ink on it and the more zeros the more value.

The value of the paper itself is nil but for some odd reason you value it. Ya can't eat money and if you were to burn it, it would be one of the most expensive sources of heat available. It is scary to admit but money is a metaphor with no real value of its own.

Money is like the Emperor's new clothes. It is more pretense and illusion than substance. Money is a metaphor. But what is it a metaphor phor?

To discover what money is a metaphor for, we won't look where most people do. We won't look at what money will buy; we will explore what money won't buy. What money will buy: a fancy car, shiny things, a new house or a vacation to Alabama are even more metaphorically delicious than money, promising us the answers to our wishes, so paradoxically they will lead us away from the hidden value of money.

The Beatles sang "Money can't buy you love" which is certainly true. But it can buy you the company of a beautiful or handsome model. It can buy you the facsimile of just about anything. It just can't buy you the intangibles that make life worth living, like happiness, joy, sadness, or ecstasy. You don't want the new car, you want the feeling you think you might get from having the new car. You don't want the new house you want the sensations you imagine you might have from owning a beautiful five bedroom roaming ranch in the best part of town. The car and the house are tangible. They are things. While what you seek is intangible, hopefully hiding behind the things. What you seek is some aspect of yourself you hope things will produce.

The primary thing that you seek and that money is a metaphor for is attention. Attention is our purely human gift. Money won't buy it and studies indicate that you can live without money but not without attention. You don't really even know exactly what attention is or how to get it. You may *want* money and all sorts of material things but what you actually *need* is attention.

How about I pay you a million dollars to spend a year in solitary confinement?

Or maybe I could just pay you 90,000 dollars to go into a job that doesn't inspire you, working for a boss you only pretend to care for with two weeks of paid vacation.

You sell yourself, your time, efforts and attention, for a metaphor. When I was young I was a designer in a factory. The factory workers would slave all week, take their paychecks and squander them on drunken binges Friday night. By Monday they were out of money again and so could justify returning to unsatisfying, demeaning work. It wasn't money they wanted. They had no idea what they wanted so they wandered fairly blindly through their lives. They were blue collar workers lacking the insight (attention focused in) to perceive themselves. Just down the street at law firms and all sorts of white collar hang outs more affluent people were doing higher class slave labor.

Attention deficit disorder is rampant in this country. We use it as an excuse. We allow people who "have" it to spend more time taking the SAT test and we suggest that people who have it should just say "yes" to some pretty fine drugs.

When someone employs you they are really only buying your attention. When someone marries you they are hedging the likelihood of getting more of your attention. Coke advertises like crazy hoping to get more of your attention than Pepsi does.

The most basic rule about money, that you just have to know if you are to discover the anatomy of money, is that money follows attention. Become a master of attention and you will never, ever, ever, ever, ever need or sell out for money again. You will have what money can't buy. When you have what money can't buy there is simply no pay-off to not having money. (Please read that last sentence again or maybe even read it a few times)

We *want* money and we *need* attention. Attention is a tiny little puff of focused awakeness. Attention is so small and so focused that it excludes nearly everything. It is our ability to focus, to pay attention to Coke instead of Pepsi, to want a BMW instead of a Ford, to be married to one person instead of everybody that gets us into trouble.

Attention is based on the economics of exclusion. Attention is all about what is left out, never really about what is included.

What you leave out haunts you. What you leave out

worries you. What you exclude also defines you. What you leave out is you hearing a wonderful party in the next room but not being invited. Attention is the place limitations begin and then reveal themselves by the metaphor of too little money: not having enough money to do what you want or, basically, not having enough money to buy absolutely everything. No matter how much money you have you can never have enough, because there is always something that you can't afford or something that isn't for sale. Money is a metaphorical solution and no matter how much metaphor you have it just isn't the real thing. This is exactly why money is always a dead end and never sufficient. The promises money makes, or the promises you make to yourself about "when I have more money..." are seldom delivered and never rewarded for long.

The Zen monk's students gathered around as he was on his death bed. His final words to them were "Give me some money."

Attention, the foundation of money, really isn't about exclusion; it is your misinterpretations about misuse of attention that have it be about limitation. You, wrongly assume that attention is limited. Attention isn't limited at all. You are an attention factory. You and every other person on the planet spin out attention constantly. Attention is not even the tiniest bit limited. It is because you perceive attention to be limited that you think there isn't enough money and that quality of life is related to money. It is because you think attention is limited that you are stingy with and can never get enough satisfaction. Our basic misunderstanding about attention and its endless abundance has us live the lie of limitations and the myth of shortage.

Discovering yourself as the source of attention and attention as the source of you and attention focused on attention as the essence of awakening that will have you easily and effortlessly discover man's best friend

Man's best friend is man. Each man, or each person is more like each other person on the planet than he or she is like anything else on Earth. The similarities between people are so great and you focus your attention on the differences between people. The fastest, easiest and most logical way to begin discovering yourself as a source of unlimited attention is to begin spreading attention around and to stop hoarding it. Get to know yourself as a creature of attention, as the source of unlimited attention on the planet and you will quickly have all the money you want. You will also stop being so busy complaining that there isn't enough time. Time is another metaphor for attention.

If you want to resolve all of your problems and eliminate suffering, if you are interested in having all the time and all the money you want, get to know yourself. Getting to know yourself is discovering what makes you truly human: attention. Attention is an evolutionary gift, money is a man made illusion. Becoming a master of attention is the meal while continuing to chase money is the menu. The menu doesn't nourish or satisfy you:

and money doesn't either.

If you want to learn more about attention and more about what it is to discover yourself as a source of attention, I invite you to come and play with me and my friends. You can begin by reading one of my books or listening to one of my seminars or coaching calls.

You can have a coaching call of your own or attend a course. Heck, you can dive into the deep end by having me come and spend two or three days with you focusing intimately and personally on how you can wake up right where you are and as you are.

Let's play! Visit www.jerrystocking.com to explore attention and wake-up.

A philosopher when you need one! He has been called the American Obi Wan Kenobi. His Light saber cuts through your stressful patterns.

Jerry Stocking is a modern day Thoreau living in the foothills of the Smoky Mountains in North Georgia with a view of our culture from the outside. Each day in his mountain retreat is an endless exploration of existence, consciousness, and feeling what it is to be a human being. Being present and mapping the terrain back to who we really are is Jerry's main occupation. His thirty-two acre farm creates an atmosphere conducive to introspection, opening, and playing, which are often lacking in our fast-paced world. Visit www.jerrystocking.com.

Are You Acting from Gratitude, Love, and Trust or Doubt and Fear?

Dr. Joe Rubino

As human beings, we operate daily reflecting a wide range of emotions with a multitude of motivations fueling our behaviors. All too often, we react emotionally to what others say or do. If our reactions are preceded by the emotions of fear, anger, or sadness, we forfeit our ability to act with personal power and effectiveness in lieu of a knee-jerk response. This reaction is all too often sourced in fear and low self-esteem. We may focus on what's wrong with us and our lives, fear being controlled, hurt, or taken advantage of. We may overlook the many things we have in our lives for which we should rightly be grateful, doubt our ability to thrive and access the abundance we see all around us in the world, reacting instead from the concern of scarcity and the expectation of failure, hurt, and disappointment. We may see ourselves in competition for the world's resources and the love and attention of others rather than realizing that there is more than enough of all that is good to go around. We forget that we manifest what we expect rather than needing to compete for limited resources.

Whenever we forget that we are magnificent beings and that there is plenty of wealth, happiness, fun, and fulfillment to go around, we might feel the need to protect ourselves from what we perceive to be a dangerous world. We likewise tend to forget that others operate from the same lacking self-confidence, scarcity of gratitude, and deficient self-love that we often do. So, whenever two or more individuals see themselves as not good enough to tap into the world's abundance and get all their needs met from a physical, social, mental, and emotional perspective, conflicts are likely to arise. The result is broken relationships, strained communication, emotional pain, struggle, and suffering. All of these are needless and optional for those who realize their ability to detach from the struggle and master their emotional response.

When we stop to realize that everyone else suffers from the same self-doubt and fear of being dominated and cheated out of getting their fair share of love, fun, money, possessions, and security, we can break the vicious cycle of endless competition and continual striving for domination. We can realize that cooperation and communication is more effective in producing harmony than competition and a focus on self-interest based on fear. We can intentionally choose to trust that others are doing the best they know how to do based upon how they see the world. We can assume that they act from good intentions, even when we fear the opposite. We can hold them as worthy, competent, loving, good natured and capable of creating win-win relationships rather than fearing them as hateful, ill meaning, incompetent, unworthy, selfish opponents.

When we decide to champion others by looking for the best in them and interact with them out of an attitude of gratitude for their gifts, strengths, and positive qualities, in such as manner that they are clear that we hold them as intrinsically good and worthy of our love and respect, we provide for them a new and exciting opportunity for them to show up for us in this manner. Our decision to hold others as great (because they really are when we strip away their anger, fears, and insecurities) allows them the freedom to rise to our expectations. By operating from love and gratitude for the wisdom and empathy we develop as a result of our interactions with others, we see their mistakes as temporary indiscretions producing valuable lessons from which to learn and grow rather than reflections of a fundamentally defective being.

The key to bringing out the best in others is non-attachment. When we realize that we have total control over our response to any situation, and we give up our right to be invalidated by others or control them, we will possess a newfound freedom that allows us to exit the drama of conflict in favor of understanding, compassion, and love. Decide now to be grateful for the challenges you will encounter in your life and business. See the problems that arise as opportunities for your personal development. Look for these challenges as you go about your day, be grateful when you encounter them, and seek out the gifts awaiting your discovery.

Exercise for Expanding Gratitude and Shifting Your Reactive Nature

1. List all the things you have decided to be grateful for in your life and business.
2. In your daily journal, record each time you fail to express gratitude for a challenging situation.
3. Catch yourself reacting emotionally to what someone says or does and shift your perception in that moment to appreciate the learning experience at hand.
4. In your daily life and business, who are you not holding as magnificent?
5. How can you champion their excellence and express gratitude for the opportunity to grow in love and wisdom that they are gifting you instead of reacting with anger, sadness, or fear?
6. Who are you seeking to control or avoid being controlled by? Will you take on the practice of non-attachment in your relationship with them by creating space for them to be who they are? Do this for 30 days and record in your journal how your

interactions with them evolve. Make note of something that you can be grateful for in each situation.

Dr. Joe Rubino is a life-changing life optimization and business coach and the best-selling creator of the SelfEsteemSystem.com and 12 transformational books available worldwide in 23 languages. To receive a complimentary audio program entitled "7 Steps to Soaring Self-Esteem" and a free 1 year membership in The Success Achievers' Club ($129 value), visit `www.theselfesteemsystem.com`. *For more information on his books, audios, and coaching program, visit* `www.centerforpersonalreinvention.com`.

The Myth of Inspiration
the Non-Metaphysical Side of Law of Attraction and Getting Things Done

Geoff Hoff

There are two meanings to the word "inspiration". One is wanting to achieve a greater good or aspire to a greater goal because of something or someone you have encountered along the way. Nelson Mandela is a good example. What he was able to do, to accomplish, despite the circumstances in his life proves what humans are capable of, given the proper amount of passion and commitment. This is inspirational. The ocean is inspirational. It is a grand and powerful example of the miracle of creation and the small, important place we have within that.

Spontaneous expressions of affection, anonymous acts of charity, conspicuous acknowledgment of good work and good deeds can inspire. Even, sometimes, chocolate cake, if it is dark and rich enough.

Most people, however, especially people who want to

get something done, use the word "inspiration" with a different meaning. They think of it as some sort of divine spark, the kiss of the Muse, whispering eloquent ideas that bypass all their mental faculties and allow them to create spontaneously. Many even wait around for this inspiration to hit, all the while producing nothing, affecting no one.

Inspiration thought of in this way is a myth.

I can hear the hoots from artists and entrepreneurs everywhere. I'm sure I will get people wanting to express to me in the most vehement terms the almost out-of-body experiences they have had when deep in the creative process. Yes. I know. I have experienced those wonderful moments, also. Or rather, not moments, they seem outside of time. When in that kind of creative state, time no longer exists for you, nor do the needs of your body, or your family. Or that noisy cat who hasn't been fed for the fourteen hours you have been under the spell of it.

This is not really inspiration. Many artists use that notion to exclude the general populace from thinking they can create art. "It is something only we special people have." Don't let them fool you. Don't let them exclude you from the club. Anyone can learn to have those experiences, whether you are an artist, an entrepreneur or someone who wants to build a better bookshelf. It is not a Muse whispering new thoughts into your ears. It is not from outside yourself. It is, instead, the flower that grows in a well-tilled garden. Those thoughts, those creations, occur because you have cleared the way for them, sometimes over a very long period of time, often without you realizing that's what you are doing. The trick is to do it consciously.

A farmer can spend years clearing the land, pulling the rocks out, softening the soil, fertilizing it with good, old-fashioned cow dung. This is the artist being educated, reading; letting other art wash over them, letting the world wash over them consciously. The farmer plants the seeds early. Some bulbs get planted years before they bloom. It can take an acorn up to a half century to produce another acorn, but that does not mean that second acorn spontaneously appeared after being whispered to by a Muse.

After the allotted time, the plants (the creation) then grow. Some of them surprise with their beauty, their strangeness, their originality, they seem effortless, but the one who is creating has worked hard for them.

The truth is that, when you have trained your mind in the proper way, it will come up with some surprising things. Observe all the time. But observe in a way that most people don't. It's a simple adjustment that anyone can make, and I recommend making it: Train yourself to notice your observations. Sometimes they then become dormant for years, bubbling and boiling in what Paul Sheele calls the "other than conscious mind." But if you hadn't noticed them consciously, they would remain external, unusable.

Let me attack it in a different way:

I was very excited when I saw the movie, *The Secret*.

It had a lot I agreed with and there was much new information in it to ponder. However, there were two things that didn't ring true.
1. They talked very little about actually doing things - as they used to say in religious circles, ya gotta be in motion, God can't steer a parked car. And...
2. The special effect in the movie representing the energetic waves emanating from the person's thoughts that bring the magic of the Universe in to play seemed really silly.

Phoowie on that, and all it's ancestors and progeny, I say. I think the Law of Attraction is much simpler and more direct than that. Stick with me, this will all come together.

Our minds are great filtering devices. We have so much input that we'd go crazy very quickly if our minds didn't filter out what wasn't needed or currently relevant. When you're in a room with lots of people, lots of conversations, you can focus in on just one of them. The others seem to disappear into a soft, only slightly distracting buzz. That doesn't mean those other conversations don't exist, it just means you aren't aware of them, you've filtered them out.

When you focus both consciously and unconsciously on something, you are training your mind to notice that something rather than some other thing. When you train your mind to notice that, it filters out things in your environment that aren't that, and makes obvious the opportunities that are that or will bring that. They seem to appear like magic. They were already there, trust me, you just didn't notice them.

Now I say "consciously AND unconsciously", and this is important. As an example that most people can relate to, if we were to concentrate on having money, visualize having money, get emotionally excited about having money, say affirmations about having money, without first acknowledging what's already there in our subconscious mind about money, (telling the truth about what we believe rather than trying to change or fix what we believe) we're just painting over the rust and the rust is what will "manifest". More specifically, it is that rust that you are still noticing, so you'll move toward more of that.

It is easy to notice the thoughts that don't support achieving what you desire, those thoughts we call negative, those thoughts we usually try to repress and resist. (Remember, that which you resist persists! What you focus on expands.) Don't resist those thoughts. Notice them. They're there, so tell the truth about that. You can even play with them. "Hey, thanks, what a great thought. You're such a genius. Now! What do I want to think?"

Acknowledge them and accept them as part of who you are. Once you do this, you are in control, not the thought. When it comes up again, (and it will) do it again. ("Hello, again! Haven't heard from you in a while. How's the wife and kids?") Then choose to reframe it.

What's "reframe"? Stop for a brief moment to acknowledge fully what's there; then suggest a new thought. It is said that "fear" and "excitement" elicit the same physical sensations, that it is only what we choose to call the feeling that makes it one or the other. When fear comes up, thank it for being there and decide to reframe it as excitement. Another example, if you often find yourself thinking "I can't", when you notice it come up again, say "Cool. You can't. Gotcha, dude!" then reframe it into, "How can I?"

It's okay to giggle a little at the thought before you reframe it, by the way.

Once you get into the habit of acknowledging what is already there and reframing it, surround yourself with images, words, people and things that support the new way of thinking.

How does this relate to inspiration, to getting things done? If we constantly observe, constantly notice what we observe, we are feeding the other than conscious mind. That part of us loves to give back, and it will rearrange those thoughts, those observations; those notions into something that seems quite new, that seems like inspiration.

You, yourself, have the responsibility for and control over the result of your mind's focus, not the Universe. It is not waves emanating out from your head. It's not the muse. It's you focusing without restraint upon what's possible. Train your mind to acknowledge and release the old patterns, the "rust", and train it to really focus on what you desire as if you already have it, and you will (magically? Hrmph) begin to move toward that goal.

(Notice I said move. You have to move. You have to take action.) You will, indeed, have attracted it.

The final piece is the simplest, but not necessarily the easiest, and that is get into the habit of "doing." Whatever your discipline is, writing, creating products, building bookshelves, starting businesses, do it. Do it all the time. Do it wrong. Make mistakes. The more you do, the more you are telling your subconscious mind what it is you want and all that stuff you've been feeding it will start to flow to you in the most amazing, magical and inspired ways.

Geoff Hoff is a best-selling fiction author and also writes about the creative process. He teaches creative writing in courses on the Internet. You can find out more at www.TipsOnWriting.net.

Blame, Shame, Guilt and Responsibility; It Is Really A Math Problem

Blame, shame, guilt and responsibility usually go together like bread and butter which is a very sad thing, as originally those words were never meant to go together in fact, just the opposite. The word responsibility was never designed to have the associations that it has today. In fact, it basically means the opposite of restriction, confinement and burden.

The word is three words in one. Most people when they try to understand break it down to only two words.

1. ABILITY TO
2. RESPOND

That is useful and yet it still does not get to the essence of what the word is conveying. Let's look at it deeper…

- At the beginning of the word is the prefix RE, which means "do over"

- At the end of the word we have 'bility' ability abbreviated which means "power to"

So before we go any further we realize this word is about the power to do something over.

The key to this word is in the middle 'spond', which comes from a Greek musical term 'sponde', meaning "to liberate, liberation"

So what we are talking about is...

"The Power to once again liberate."

How did such a wonderful and exciting idea become associated with the horrible ideas and consequences it has today in our society?

The answer may surprise you. It is really a math problem... What do I mean? It is the problem of the word "to" (2) and the word "for" (4). Society has miss interpreted these two little words and caused a word that was meant to excite and energize to be received with dread, sadness and apprehension. Here is where the rub comes in...

- The Individual is responsible to and for oneself
- The Individual in ONLY responsible **to** (not for) others (including spouse, children, bosses, friends, society)
- When the individual attempts to take

responsibility FOR any other human being the word begins to imprison instead of liberate.

As one Master Teacher once said...
Our Diversity Supports Our Individual Freedoms... While our societies continue to try to dictate and enforce human behavior to please the majority – because of our diversity, it continues to be an uncomfortable struggle that, again and again, falls of its economic weight. There simply is not enough money in the world to buck the natural currents of individual freedom and independence of thought.

SUCCESS AND YOUR LIFE

Connie Ragen Green

You can achieve any success that you want to in your life. You may not believe that to be true, but I will show you how to make this work for you. When I was growing up my mother always told me I could be anything I wanted to be when I was an adult. I honestly did not know what she meant.

As I got older, life became more and more challenging, and I completely forgot, or at least put out of my mind, what my mother had said. By the time I was about twelve years old, I was resigned to the fact that other people could have what they dreamed about in life, but that I would have to work hard for anything I wanted in life.

As I was approaching my fiftieth birthday, I thought back to what mother had said so many times. I even asked her if she remembered saying that to me. I thought she would probably tell me she had just said those things to make me feel better, but I was mistaken.

My mother said that she had told me I could have or be anything I wanted because that is the truth. After fifty years of living I still did not understand what she meant. That conversation, more than two years ago now, has led to my understanding that it is true - you can be, do, or have anything you want in life. There are no contingencies or stipulations to this. If you want it, it is yours. That is the key: ask for what you want and it will begin to work its way towards you very quickly.

I have attempted several times to write a book on this topic, but it never seems to come out right. Yes, there are secrets, but so many people now know them that they cannot be considered secrets any longer. We live in an abundant world. Yet, when you look around you so many people seem to be struggling with money, relationships, physical conditions, and personal satisfaction in their lives. You need to know that it doesn't have to be that way in your life.

It is possible for you to have anything you want in your life. You may feel like it is impossible to have all the money you would like, be in perfect health, have the relationship of your dreams, or attain some other goal, but the truth is that you can have any of these things. Follow these three steps to attain your life goals.

1. Write down exactly what you want in your life. Be specific. If you want more money, write down the exact figure. Ask yourself by what date you would like to have this amount of money. If you would

like to have a great relationship, write down all of the details. Describe the person in as much detail as possible. What kind of clothes are they wearing? What color are their eyes? How will you feel when you have what you want? By writing down on paper exactly what you want, when you want it, and how it will make you feel when you have it, you are solidifying your intention.

2. Make a list of the reasons you do not already have these things that you are wanting in your life so deeply. Even if you know it will seem silly when you look at your list later, go ahead and write down all of your reasons. You will find out later that the majority of these reasons are not true. Many of you will write that you are not smart enough or do not deserve great things in your life. You are being very unfair to yourself if you believe these things. We are all good enough to have the exact and specific things in our life that we are dreaming of.

3. Spend a few minutes every morning with your eyes closed, thinking about how it will feel when your life it just as you want it. Imagine that everything is already the way you want it to be and that you have all of the material things, spiritual feelings, and love that you could ever imagine having in your life. Picture the details of this exclusive, beautiful life. Do this for as long as you can each morning.

If you are able to follow these three steps regularly you will see your life begin to change very rapidly. Events, people, and circumstances will come into your daily experience as if my magic. You will look back at your former life with amazement that you were willing to live that way for so much of your life. All of us have the ability and desire to live the life of our dreams.

And now I invite you to learn more about achieving the success you have only dreamed of by visiting www.SuccessAndYourLife.com and begin to live the life you deserve immediately.

Connie Ragen Green has been making money online since 2006, and now makes a comfortable mid 5 figure monthly income, primarily from her own programs and courses, information products, and affiliate marketing. She teaches you how to write short reports and articles, as well as how to set up your own blog, set up mini-sites, use Twitter and Facebook, create info products, and write your own web sales copy, which is copywriting for the Internet.

Her motto is: "If I can do it, YOU can do it!" Visit Connie at www.conniegreen.com.

Want To Make More Money Last Year?

Wendy Down

The Consciousness Playground is a membership community where Consciousness Pioneers connect (online, by teleclass and audio, and energetically) to discover, practice, and share astounding new "quantum-style" ideas and endeavors.

One of the areas we have explored is changing the past, as a way of altering our present experience. The idea that the future is created from the present is universally accepted as a fundamental truth. It is equally true, however, that the past is created from the present.

Quantum physics has demonstrated that everything—both our perceived past and future—is created from the present moment. It's a wonderful theory, you may be thinking, but how could I put that idea to practical use? I'll offer you a counter-question, one that could hardly be more practical: Would you like to make more money last year?

I will share the story that prompted this topic, and then guide you through a process of recreating your past—shifting you into a past in which you made measurably more money than your memory at the moment has evidence to show that you did.

The story began at the end of 2009 when I opened my day planner and saw, at the end of December, a dollar figure penciled in my handwriting. I remembered that I had written the number at the beginning of the year as my intention for the amount of money I wanted to make in 2009. As I saw the figure, I compared it to what I thought I had made that year, feeling a wave of disappointment because I had fallen short of my goal by a significant amount. It occurred to me that I could make the 2009 goal my intention for 2010.

Then, I noticed on my desk the book, *Blueprint for Change: A Message from Our Future*, authored by the channeled personality Bashar through Darryl Anka. (The book is available through the Bashar website, www.bashar.org, and is a very worthwhile investment.) This passage struck me profoundly:

> *"The present is not the result of the past; the present is a result of what you think it is. If you think your present is a result of your past, then that is the effect you are creating. But you are creating it now. You create the past from the present, not the other way around. Therefore, you are creating from now any so-called idea of the past, just as you are creating from now any so-called idea*

of the future. Either can be anything you desire them to be."

I thought, Wow—I wonder if, rather than increasing my income next year, I still could increase last year's? I hadn't done anything like that before, and it felt exciting. If I could change that piece of my past, then any part of my past must be changeable—including childhood memories, and the injury I'd had a few years ago.

Next, I took some practical steps to bring out the experience of a "new" past and place me in the mindset to allow this shift to happen for me. First, I got into the feeling place of believing that the dollar figure in my day planner was an accurate indicator of my 2009 income, even though it hadn't seemed to be a few weeks earlier. Second, I recalled watching a video where author Frank Kinslow (originator of the Quantum Entrainment process) demonstrates how to make your finger grow, simply by measuring one finger length against another. It's a simple process that can be done in the normal waking state of consciousness. The idea is that when something is misaligned and you simply put yourself into pure awareness, the misalignment—the chaos—is corrected. The process works with virtually everyone, even those with strongly rational beliefs.

Within a month after I did the process I will share with you, I received a check for exactly ten times the amount I had identified that I was short by! It was from the sale of a business in which I was a silent partner. I'd known I would receive some money from the sale at some point, but wasn't aware of the amount. The fact that it was precisely ten times as much as the amount I had fallen short by, and that it had been assigned to me in 2009, was amazing! I had, indeed, succeeded in making more money last year.

Here is the basic process I used to change my past, which can be applied to anything you want to alter, not just money.

1. Identify a number that is a fairly accurate assessment of what you believe your income was last year. (If you are working with a different topic, identify the reality that currently seems true but that you would prefer to be different.)

2. Choose a number that represents your desired income. Pick a figure you believe is attainable, perhaps asking yourself questions like, "What is the amount of money the person I know myself to be now deserves? How much do I deserve to make, if I allowed myself to have that and everyone around me agreed?" Pick a figure that feels somewhat out of reach, but not too much so. You can adjust it later if you want. Write down the number. (If working with a topic other than finances, identify a state that represents in measurable terms the shift that you want to make.)

3. Acknowledge that the "version" of you that has the higher income already exists, and is just as real as the version of you that you have perceived until now. The version of you that made that higher income

already has a living Universe, with evidence that supports that reality.

4. You will have the experience of "sliding into" that version of you—now. I'll offer some suggestions to help you find your desired state and become congruent with it. Recognize that the desired version of you is so present, so eager to be expressed, so ready to flood you with awareness of its presence that the only thing required of you is to just let that happen.

If you can imagine yourself making that dollar figure, and hold that possibility in your mind (or hold the idea of yourself having your desired state)—if you can access that, it is available to you. You are already there, and can simply allow that part of you to more fully express itself.

A practical way to access your desired state is to ask yourself questions such as, "How would I feel if I made that much money last year?" Let yourself say definitively in your mind: "I made this amount," and then notice the changes in what you perceive and how you feel.

Ask yourself questions like, "If that were true, how would my body hold itself differently?" and then let your body do what it would do if you were that person. How would you hold your head and shoulders? You may feel some of those shifts happening already.

Answer other questions that might be pertinent, such as: What would you be wearing? What might you eat? What inner patterns or thoughts or worries would no longer be relevant? What would be let go? What might you be spending time doing that's different or new?

What is gone, and what has replaced it?

Images or thoughts may come to you, or they may not. The changes occurring may be noticeable only in subtle ways. Simply let be what is there. At this point, even just contemplating the possibility; notice that you are not the same person you were a minute ago. There is something new and different about you now. Place your attention and awareness on that new state. It could be comfortable or uncomfortable, profound or incredibly subtle.

Just notice that, in this moment, you are fully being someone new. And, because all of reality is a reflection of who you are, your entire reality has shifted as well. Your mind may want to start analyzing what occurred; just observe it with amusement—minds do that! Notice how effortless it was to be new.

A factor to be aware of is that a few minutes ago, you were recreating yourself to be someone who has habitual patterns on this topic from the past. You had repetitive experiences, frustrations, anxieties, expectations, thought patterns, and memories about money and income.

Those patterns reflect who you were just a short while ago. In this moment, you have the absolute authority to choose: Instead of creating yourself as someone who has habitual patterns from the past, you can be someone who has no undesired habitual patterns regarding money and income.

As you entertain that possibility, you might notice your mind trying to control or understand. Whatever is passing through your experience simply let yourself be aware of who you are now, and fully be that. Allow any feelings or thoughts to move through you without resistance. As you are aware of these experiences, the power of your awareness works to organize the energy that is expressing itself as thoughts, feelings, beliefs, and history; reorganizing them in a way that reflects and resonates with who you are now.

There is nothing to do but notice, enjoy, and be present to what is showing up in your experience now. Any misalignments not resonant with who you are in this moment will yield to the incredible organizing power of who you truly are: pure awareness of the zero-point field. They will shift from their pervious phase to one that is more resonant.

Regardless of what shows up, expand your awareness beyond those experiences. They are not happening to you; they are happening within the framework of who you really are: unlimited potential. The energy is like dough, easily shaped into something new.

In this moment, as you experience being consciousness itself, consider the truth that your past has nothing at all to do (in a controlling way) with what you are experiencing now and who you are now. There is nothing to do other than be who you are in this moment. The consciousness that is you organizes everything around you.

Now, let pop into your awareness something the version of You who made that income last year—the version of You that you want to be—will do when you finish this process. It could be something you'd been waiting to do, something you'd let go of, something you'd say, or something you'd buy.

And now, imagine what it would feel like to do that thing. Try it out in your imagination, so you can work out any nuances. Feel that action or non-action as simply an expression of the feeling you are being, the natural outflow of this You.

When you are ready, open your eyes and see what the room looks like through the eyes of the person who resonates with that income or that desired state. Notice that the entire space actually reverberates with that same You. It's all new; it's all different; it's all a reflection that contains the new You, singing itself back in response to you.

Are you willing to take a specific action today as that person, as the new You? Actually acting as that person grounds that You into 3D reality.

After making this sort of change, something to expect is what Bashar calls "The Echo." When you have altered your state of being, a reflection of the previous state may show up one more time. It is as if you were standing in a canyon, yelling the word, "Red," and then you changed and started yelling, "Green." You would hear an echo of the word "Red" one more time before you started hearing echoes of "Green."

If a reflection of the old version of reality shows up, that is your opportunity "lock in" the new version by responding differently than you would have previously.

This time, you will know it is a temporary manifestation that does not need to be repeated, and you can respond accordingly.

A second suggestion is to be willing to start by seeing, accepting, and celebrating even the tiniest piece of evidence, including being willing to feel silly about what you see as evidence. Sometimes, all it takes to pave the way for a major shift is something small. Notice it, accept it, and believe it, and then bigger things will show up.

A third suggestion is to choose something physical that represents the version of you that you prefer to be. Recently I recommended that a client of mine buy new underwear that represents the person she wants to be. Another idea is that carrying a stone in your left pocket means you are being the old you, and switching it to the right pocket represents the new you. Taking physical actions with conscious intent can "ground" the new version of you, making it easier to live in this You from here on.

At times you may still find yourself reaching for the old, familiar state. Right after you've made a shift, both states are close enough to be easily accessible, and a momentary lapse is insignificant. Over time, you will find it natural to maintain the new state and will become accustomed to it.

Congratulations, you have just changed your past! Enjoy the experiences that having a higher income or other preferred state brings.

Here is a link to an audio-recording in which I will guide you step-by-step through the "Make More Money

Last Year" process that I used myself:

www.consciousnessplayground.com/store/audio-want-to-make-more-money-last-year

Also, if you enjoy exploring metaphysical concepts like this changing your past in a way that yields results, join the Consciousness Playground where we do this all the time: www.consciousnessplayground.com.

As an award-winning Life Coach, teacher and pioneer in the field of consciousness, Wendy Down has been actively inspiring people to a higher expression of themselves since 1999.

*She has taken her uncanny ability to discover untapped individual and collective potential and created a thriving private coaching practice and The Consciousness Playground,(*www.consciousnessplayground.com*) an online community.*

The Root of All Evil

Most often when someone claims to be using critical thinking they are simply criticizing, being critical instead of doing critical problem solving. One of the reasons problem solving skills and creative thinking are left out of the mix and critical problem solving winds up being criticism is because of something very, very basic. It starts when we make a judgment instead of calibrating. And a judgment is the very beginning of your BS-Belief System. All a BS-Belief System is; is a bunch of judgments about things that are still moving.

So what is wrong with judging? It depends on if you have what you want to have and if you are being who you want to be or doing what you want to do. The problem with making a judgment is when you do, you have formed an opinion or come to a conclusion. And the BIG issue with that is Life does not stop moving and it constantly changes. And as my Grampa Vetter said, "A judgment, just like your BS-Belief System, is where you have stopped thinking."

There are even famous books, most every spiritual

tradition has something very similar, out there that has a quote that most people seem to ignore or justify themselves around...

"Judge not, least ye be not judged."
Holy Bible – King James Version

Another problem with judgment is it gives one the false sense that the decision they have come to in their mind, is accurate for the outside world. To attempt to change and create your future financial situation based on personal judgment is simply BS-Belief System and it causes one to be way off the mark.

So what should some use instead?

How about...calibration!!!!!

Both judging and calibrating do the same things...

- Evaluate
- Decide
- Measure
- And that is where they stop being similar

The differences between the two are earth shattering. The biggest difference is that judging holds one in prison and calibrating sets one free. Let's compare the two, shall we? *(see table 2, p. 103)*

The US stock market has even put out a warning about this. "Past performance is no guarantee of future performance."

Judgment	Calibration
stops thinking	continues thinking
is about the past	about the future
do not allow adjustments	encourages adjustments
permanent	temporary
measures the future based on the past	measures the future based on where you are
criticizes	reserves judgment
out of alignment with the universe	in line with the universe
strictly internal	uses both the internal and external

Table 2

Judgment energy is created by making a decision of defeat. It takes a specific calibration situation; personalizes it and generalizes that one calibration incident to other calibration situations that are not similar but are perceived as similar.

Judgments are useful for things that are repetitive opening doors, sitting on chairs, putting gas in the car, etc. They are less than useful in situations with other variables such as the energy of other people and situations are a part of the mix.

Calibrations are useful for everything else. As an example judgment makes us think we know the answer and have it down where calibration causes us to continue to compare life and what we are creating so we get to create better and better stuff. (Money, Health, Relationships, Happiness, etc.)

One of the reasons the movie *The Secret* was such a success and sold a lot of copies is because it brought a new judgment, i.e. a new belief that people could agree or disagree with. The real secret of creation and life is about calibration, not a law.

The real secret that the movie *The Secret* did not tell you will probably surprise you. First the movie confuses you by telling you that the Law of Attraction is the secret. The trouble with that is LOA is a law and it doesn't matter if you know about it or if you don't. Even if the laws of attraction were a secret to you it would not matter one single bit. Now you may be thinking, "How can this be true? Where do you get off saying that?"

Bear with me here just a little bit and you'll see it clearly. Let me ask you, "How does gravity work?" and then ask yourself, "If I didn't mentally know about gravity would I float off the planet? If I didn't know about gravity could I walk off the edge of The Empire State Building and not go down?" Think about it for a minute, what value does focusing on the law of gravity have? It is what it is and it works how it works.

When we answer those questions honestly we realize, whether or not we know about gravity, what it is or how it works; we are always subject to gravity as long as we are where it is. In other words we never break the law (theory) of gravity we only demonstrate it. And if there was no gravity there would be no reason to discover the theory of lift so we could build planes that use thermosdynamics and lift to use gravity to fly.

Think about it for a minute, what value does focusing on the law of gravity have? It is what it is and it works how it works. The same is true for the law of attraction.

Now that we have cleared that up a little let's look at what the real secret is. To understand the real secret there are a few understandings that must first take place.

- The first is that everything is energy.
- Energy moves by vibrational frequencies.
- Energy moves between energy poles.
- Your five (5) senses are vibrational interpreters.
- Every Human Being (You) is made up of two energy poles.

Before we go into what the real secret is let's remember how energy poles work. Energy travels in vibrational frequency waves between poles. When poles are aligned the energy flows uninterrupted. When the poles are misaligned the energy flow is disrupted. A term we are familiar with is: there is a short in the electrical system which means some poles somewhere are out of alignment.

Emotionally when poles are out of alignment there is compulsion which usually leaves one feeling dis-empowered and vulnerable. In other words it feels bad. When poles are aligned it produces choice or freedom. It feels good. So you see this is all about compulsion or choice.

So now we get to the real secret and that is every human being is made up of two poles or as my Grampa

Vetter says "two ends of the same stick". The real secret is about continually aligning the two poles that make up who you are. This requires calibration instead of judgment.

The first pole you are really familiar with. It's "the you", you think you are; the one with all the beliefs, judgments and rules about who you are and who you are not, about what's right and what's wrong. The second pole that makes up the totality of you, when combined with who you think you are is who you really are. Simply, there is 'who you think you are' and 'who you really are' and energy flows between them.

The pole you are not very familiar with is wise, healthy, smart, and totally powerful and makes up about 90% of you and likes to do all the work. The pole you are aware of (who you think you are) gets confused stressed, fearful, feels powerless and not sure of yourself or decisions. And yet even though this aspect of you is only about 10% of who you really are, it tries to do all the work.

Now the real secret is really worth paying attention to and learning how to align the two poles, because the real secret is very liberating when you understand the real secret is… You are the leading edge extension of Divinity. There is you and there is Divinity, the same stick, not separate, the same thing in different poles and when you align the poles lookout cause then you start really living life and getting what you want.

The root of all evil (live backwards) has nothing to do with love or money, it is not being aware that there are two aspects of you and when they are aligned everything in your life moves with ease and flow. Mis-alignment of those two aspects of you is the root of all backward live(ing).

The Easiest Way To Have Money Flow To You

Win Winger is the author of *The Einstein Factor* and developer of Imaging Streaming and has a Think Tank program designed to developing problem solving solutions by applying his focus of attention on problem solving…problem solving. In doing this Win and his people have come up with some amazing solutions including for children in school to reclaiming the eroding beaches around the world.

In a conversation with some people about which of these Conscious, Subconscious, SuperConscious to use and how to access them, Win suggested why not use all of them. Below is part of the conversation.

Win,

I agree why not all of them and the answer to that is not where you would think it is.

What do I mean by that? Well most people think to get in contact with Conscious, Subconscious and/or Unconscious PLUS Super-conscious it starts and stays pretty much in the brain. WARNING, WARNING, WARNING. About to fall off a deep ledge.

Others might think it is in the mind. (Of course it depends on where one says the mind is etc.) CAUTION, CAUTION, CAUTION

Some others might say, heart, it's in your heart. Alert, Alert, Alert (And it would really depend on what one means when they say heart. Most people point to the middle of their chest and what they are actually referring to are emotions (call it the emotional brain or emotional mind) but the one thing we do know is it is usually in opposition the head brain/mind.

I propose the place to allow money to flow to you is not in the brain, nor in what most refer to as heart.

Some might say the reason the head and heart are at odds often is because one's left and right hemisphere's are not balanced (using one more than the other) or some might say the conscious and (un)subconscious are not aligned.

I will not disagree with those metaphors and yet I suspect they keep people focused in the one particular area that is less than useful.

What area is that you ask?

Head Space!

Head Space is where you head brain (logical, focus, etc) and what most people mean when they refer to their heart, i.e. heart brain (emotive feelings) continue to push against each other as both have a charge around them, a charge that hooks you into a position that often is hard to get out of. It is the energy charge that holds our BS-Belief System in place. And it is the energy patterns of our BS-Beliefs Systems that slow down the speed at which we get, gather, give and/or hold on to money.

What happens when people say, "that person is coming from their head or that person is coming from their heart" is actually different displays of Head Space. (The energy field – torsion field) that generates charge that hooks or blocks one from getting what you want.

Now the actuality is coming from Head Space is not a bad thing as there is only one of two places one can operate from. BUT you raised the question of getting the Conscious, Subconscious and Superconscious to work together and all at the same time, instead of seemingly at different times. Head Space, because of its' very nature segregates and separates these things out so they are experienced independently of each other, not collectively.

Given what you want to accomplish and achieve, all levels of consciousness working together in unison, it cannot and will not be experienced from Head Space, in other words, from thinking.

There is another torsion field that is on average 30 feet wide spinning and turning around every single individual on the planet (think big donut with a small center) and the center of that big donut runs from about the middle of your chest (right at the top of the physical heart) and extends down to about two inches (2") below the belly-button.

That particular torsion field I have dubbed, trademarked and now call HeartSpace™ (learn more at www.beyondclearing.com)!

There is a specific place in that center column that is the core of it all and from that specific place.

Conscious, Subconscious and Superconscious ALL work together including what most term the head and the heart.

The trick or the key or the secret (whatever you want to call it) of HeartSpace™ is there is zero hooking charge.

Did you read that correctly? Zero hooking charge

Do you get what that means?

All those things that used to bother you, all those things that charged you up, all those feelings of pressure GONE, NO LONGER THERE. True FREEDOM!

The cool thing about HeartSpace™ is you can experience EVERY SINGLE EMOTION, GOOD AND BAD, and not get hooked by any of them. If you do, it simply means you have moved back into Head Space and that's not a bad thing (since there are only two places you can be).

This is beyond clearing all the limited and

limiting blocks and beliefs in your subconscious this is by-passing them.

Yes, it takes practice just like riding a bike or walking or driving took practice and when you play with it enough it's really, really cool, fun and exciting.

Imagine the sublime feeling of peace, joy, happiness, safety, comfort, inclusion, bliss carrying you without pushing you or giving you the charge that you had to have it.

One of the 1st times I used this with a client, he was what could be called very analytical-left brained person and yet he was a owner of a specific type of therapeutic massage company called SET (Structural Energetic Therapy?) he came in with a yellow legal pad filled with 16-18 pages of questions about how to do a particular modality he was learning called Matrix Energetics. Once he got into HeartSpace™ I had him go through every single question on every single page and he had the answer to every one of them. He said nothing needed clearing now as everything was clear, thus beyond clearing. (Actually, the questions no longer had any charge so they were no longer important) and from then on he uses Matrix in his practice with ease.

From HeartSpace™ all the 'yeah buts' about money are gone, all the 'I can'ts', all the 'I don't know if I cans' and all the statements that hold a charge no longer hook you and then things start changing for you. And just like walking or talking or driving once we practice and play with HeartSpace™ long enough it becomes a natural as breathing. (www.beyondclearing.com)

Conclusion

Here you have it, different levels and different views and different way to look at and deal with money in ways that are uniquely opposite of the way most people look at money. These people have a relationship with money that makes it a non-issue in their lives and they are able to live comfortable and to help others in numerous ways that the average person can not.

Wouldn't you like the same opportunity as these people? Well this whole book has been designed to be a dance among our Sacred Cows. In other words the dance of shifting our BS-Belief Systems to allow us the flexibility to improve our 'Inner Game', since there can be no outer game unless the inner game is played.

Your Inner Game is the only game there is to play. Enlightenment is an inside job and as one of our authors said in one of his books, *Enlightenment is Losing Your Mind* and most of the authors here agree, money really isn't real. We put way to much spin on something that is really simply.

The way to break free from the money game is let

your sacred cows dance and then you have peace, joy, happiness AND Money. And that is what you really want, isn't it?

Testimonials

Here are some of the typical testimonials I get from helping people.

I got a call from a woman who told me because of my help and suggestions she no longer has hot flashes and her menopause is under control now.

A lady called with Lupus and after meeting with her within fifteen minutes her pain was almost gone.

Before working with Dr. Vetter:

My life was defined by a pronounced, regular mood swing into an extreme depression. When I was not depressed, I just tried to get as much done as I could so that I would be supported when it happened again. I avoided making commitments because I couldn't count on myself to be "up to it" emotionally.

Now:

I am on an even keel, learning to trust myself to be reliable and predictable. I can make plans in the future now that I know I will be fine! I am also more active day-to-day and not pushing myself into over-productive behaviors just because I am having "a good day".

Lorriane D., Friendswood, TX

I got a call from a family where the husband had, had esophageal cancer (throat) and could not eat or swallow. After having his wife spray a particular product on his throat, back of his neck, chest and feet in three days he was able to eat and drink again (now taking the product orally) and she called to report they had just been to their MD and he said whatever they had been doing to keep it up because it looked like the cancer was now in remission.

I had someone call me who's doctor had put them on dialysis because he had 4% kidney function. Three months later they were talking about taking him off dialysis (unheard of) and that his kidney function was up to 40% now. We just did some emotional work on his feelings toward his parents and he is feeling even better than before.

A while back we had a client call from the ICU of MD Anderson Cancer Center. His doctor had just given him a hospice card and told him to prepare for the inevitable (croaking). We found an answer that was not expected (a product that addressed his specific need) and we got it to his wife. She gave him 3 ounces one day and four the next. The next day they moved him out of ICU to a regular room. # or 4 ounces the next day and the following day the same. On the fourth day they did blood work and sent him home as his blood showed the cancer to be going in to remission. On the fifth day we called his house and his wife said he wasn't there, he was out shopping.

Have a friend in Virginia would has had 11 surgeries on his knees and back. Has a rod in one leg and steel pins in one of his feet. He is an ole' rough and tough construction brick mason from way back. He could not go up the stairs without a lot of pain. After three days of following directions he could go up and down the stairs with very little pain. Within two weeks he was able to jog with his kids.

And this is the most interesting part.. There are no more problems.. There is no more hour after hour of self analysis.. No-one to analyze.. No-one to observe.... There are a few tears maybe once a week now, rather than 4 or 5 times a day.. And those tears are of release and joy from acceptance of my own okness.

From a letter from Mary J., Charlotte, N.C.

Someone attempted to control me over a situation.. I simply let things go.. it just doesn't matter any more. It doesn't occur to me to be grasping or competitive and consequently, things seem to come towards me quite naturally of their own accord...

Marisa L., London, England

In my daily life, there is no stress.. I have a huge amount of work to do at present, yet it warrants no emotional response, whereas before, even the thought of it, brought on massive levels of anxiety, panic and emotional negativity and physiological pain. Now, nothing… absolutely nothing. In every situation, I am calm and I take everything in my stride.

Betty M., Memphis, TN

There is actually a sense of loss... no more do I have any internal mental/emotional voices.. Its strange in a way.. I am almost lonely.. the lifelong vocal companions have gone.. no tormenters.. no voice of conscience.. no inner analyst.. no inner critic... no duality of me and the Universe.. and unless I really go there, there is even no observer and the observed.. it's all so empty.. oh, it's so impossible to explain.. LOL.

J.C. Honolulu, HI

It's weird.. a lifetimes pattern of thinking and beliefs no longer apply... It's the little things which bring this home to me.. e.g.... When I used to find my parking space there waiting for me, I used to say "Thank you Universe." Now I tend to think "The Universe isn't other.... What am I talking to.. It's all me anyway." There is nowhere to go. The buck stops here. I am all there is. Without beginning and end. I am creator.

Ms. Shirley A., Augusta, GA

Life and loss are two sides of the same coin.. Male/female... up/down... past/future.. internal/external.. sadness and joy.. I find no difference. And this has become my natural state of being.. to attempt to think of opposites or polarities is nonsensical and quite puzzling and it simply won't compute inside my head.. so I'm thinking a lot less too. :)) Hmm.. do I really want to recreate a dualistic reality?

As the observer, I am.. I am an awareness typing.. last night awareness was sadness.. awareness was crying at the sense of loss.. yet how can one lose anything when one is everything.. ah the rub of it.. integration is as easy as it is complex.. ;-)

Kathy B., Houston, TX

With no me, no others, with only pure awareness, what is the 'reality' in spiritual guides, teachers, helpers, dead people.. as a professional psychic and medium for such entities, this has been a lifelong belief system.. as well as being an experiential one.. I can't even begin to get my head around that subject yet..

Sally S, Oklahoma City, OK

My energy level is fine. rather than expending energy worrying about this, fretting about that.. I simply get on with what is in front of me.. as nothing else actually exists for me beyond that..

Mike W, San Diego, CA

Yes... There is also the realization that the buck stops here. I am the decision maker. Empowered... I 100% know that I am that power, own that power, and what ever I do... is using that power. It cannot be any other way.

Robert J., Sussex, England

Enlightenment is alone and all-One. The loneliness comes from the loss of my inner dialogue. My mind now seeks new input, rather than creating its own.

Jesse M., Spring Hill, TN

I do not know how you will feel... I know now that I am complete simply by being me.. I do not need another as a reflection or projection of myself.. I do not need to search outside of myself for anything.

Larry D., Pasadena, TX

Resources

Join Houston on Facebook www.facebook.com/likedocresults.

Join Houston on Twitter www.twitter.com/docresults.

We have designed many ways to get you personal help from Houston. If you want help here are a few of the ways to receive it.

To receive your FREE copy of *Train Your Thinking, The Power Portal for Long-Lasting Success* visit www.TrainYourThinking.com.

For more articles and to stay in touch with this information visit www.DocResults.com/blog.

Click here to find out about all three levels of HeartSpace™, Level 1 is the fastest stress reliever process in the world. Level 2 sets up it up so that business and personal relationships work with ease and flow and Level 3 is the fastest way to glimpse an experience of spiritual enlightenment.

To learn about *This One Secret* which is the answer to your questions and the solution to your problems, visit www.ThisOneSecret.com.

If you want to take part in an e-coaching program that is out of this world, visit www.secretsuccess.com.

To get personal healing on any of these levels…

Spiritual, Mental, Emotional, Physical, Financial or Relational visit www.docresults.com/healing.

To get personal Spiritual Transformation visit www.docresults.com/spiritual-transformation.

To get more information on using our Business Intuitive Services visit www.docresults.com/business-intuitive.

To get more information on using our Personal Individual Intuitive Services visit www.docresults.com/individual-intuitive.

Or to find out more about our Mentor/Miracles Coaching Program visit www.docresults.com/mentor-miracles-coaching.

About the Author

Houston Vetter is the proud Founder and CEO of BalancedLivingMagazine.com, the world's leading magazine and website for the empowerment of you the individual. Houston is very proud to be your advocate for a balanced life of ease and flow of health, wealth and relationships filled with joy and wonder. Houston's passion is to be a catalyst to help people know who they really are and is willing to start by coming along side right where you are and encourage and support you to get what it is you really want. He has Master level skills in over 35 different modalities including some Piled Higher and Deepers. As one international trainer once said, "He has more letters behind his name than alphabet soup, and if he can't help you get what you want, you might want to check and make sure you're not six feet under."

Houston's other projects include being an author of 10 books, including *Train Your Thinking, The Power Portal For Long-Lasting Success*. He is the creator and publisher of many break-through self-empowering products @ www.DocResults.com, speaker, seminar leader, trainer and Master Teacher. He is also the Managing Director of the FBI-Feel Better Institute for the last 25 years.

Believe it or not, Houston has lived in Houston, TX for the last 18 years and helped found and works with "God's Strong Tower Ministries", a 501(c)(3) organization, that focuses on providing support, including a half-way home for Veterans of our Armed Services. He also is a regular feature guest on a syndicated business CBS radio in Houston and Dallas, TX giving tips on how to use your 'Inner Game' in Business, called "Talking Business". The host of the show says, "We like Dr. Vetter because he makes the woo-woo practical. And he has a great tag-line too, 'To Feel Better, Call Dr. Vetter.'

Notes

Notes

www.ingramcontent.com/pod-product-compliance
Lightning Source LLC
Chambersburg PA
CBHW070814100426
42742CB00012B/2356